Why Did God Give My Kids Free Will?

Why Did God Give My Kids Free Will?

He Could've Waited until They Moved Out

Ken Swarner

DAVID C COOK

transforming lives together

WHY DID GOD GIVE MY KIDS FREE WILL?
Published by David C Cook
4050 Lee Vance Drive
Colorado Springs, CO 80918 U.S.A.

Integrity Music Limited, a Division of David C Cook
Brighton, East Sussex BN1 2RE, England

The graphic circle C logo is a registered trademark of David C Cook.

The website addresses recommended throughout this book are offered as a
resource to you. These websites are not intended in any way to be or imply an
endorsement on the part of David C Cook, nor do we vouch for their content.

Details in some stories have been changed to protect
the identities of the persons involved.

Library of Congress Control Number 2022933387
ISBN 978-0-8307-8419-6
eISBN 978-0-8307-8420-2

The Team: Susan McPherson, Jeff Gerke, James Hershberger,
Jack Campbell, Susan Murdock
Cover Design: Micah Kandros
Cover Photo: Shutterstock

Printed in the United States of America
First Edition 2022

1 2 3 4 5 6 7 8 9 10

052622

Dedicated to my family—thanks for
letting me share these stories!

Contents

Author's Note

"Be still, and know that I am God."

That line from Psalm 46:10 has seen my wife and me through a number of parental challenges.

Humor has helped a lot too.

I am not a theologian. I don't work in a church, and I've never authored a serious work on Christianity. But I have been on the front lines of parenting for a very long time, and I have lived to laugh about it. I have been with the same woman for more than thirty-eight years. I have four children, two grandchildren, a dog, and a cat. I am a Christian. I have also been a PTA president, school board member, Cub Scout leader, soccer coach, and classroom volunteer. And once, I built a homework jail.

In the following pages, I share stories from my ministry as a father and husband with quick, sixty-second Christian reflections in each chapter. If you finish the book and feel a little less stressed as a parent, maybe even inspired a little more as a Christian, then I will have fulfilled my mission.

Blessings!

CHAPTER ONE

What Is God's Plan for Imperfect Parents?

It's amazing how many moms and dads believe they are terribly imperfect parents. They are worried, stressed, self-conscious, and guilt-ridden about it, to the point where they doubt their natural instincts and can even lose their faith in God.

Who decides who is perfect anyway? Where do we even get terms like that? Certainly, God discovered that His children, Adam and Eve, weren't flawless, and yet He still managed to get through the eternities. So why does it bother us so much that our lives get messy and people know it?

Probably because we all know "perfect" parents, right? Those moms and dads who are well-groomed and stable, with impeccable little children who are neatly dressed, fold their hands piously in the pew, get good grades, and don't burp the words to the National Anthem at the ballpark. But seriously, do we want to be like those people?

Heck yeah!

And yet, here we are ... far from perfect, trying to take measure of God's plan for us, and wondering why it always seems to include poor report cards and nasty notes from the Sunday school teacher.

It certainly reminds me of that time my wife came home ranting after she'd taken our son to the doctor for his annual physical. It took a while to understand her, but in so many words, she said, "We have to find a new pediatrician."

Why does it bother us so much that our lives get messy and people know it?

I patted the seat next to me and asked her to sit down. "Okay, sweetheart, why do we need to find a new doctor?"

She drew in a deep breath. "I took our son to get his physical."

"And?"

"And when the nurse told our son to strip down to his socks and underwear, she gasped."

"Because she's never seen a boy in his underwear?"

"No, because your son was wearing socks that belong in a compost bin."

I cringed.

"I don't think he's changed them for a week," she continued with tears forming in her eyes. "I forgot to check before we left home."

I held her hand. "Are you feeling badly because the nurse said something to you?"

She nodded.

"What did she say?"

"I don't know—I couldn't understand her with her hand over her nose."

I smiled. "Okay, so they were dirty. That's not the end of the world, is it?"

She shook her head. "The dirt wasn't nearly as bad as his big toe sticking through his sock."

I winced. "What about the other sock?"

"You mean the one that looked like a flip-flop?"

I stood up and paced the room. "So what happened next?"

"The nurse asked if our son would be more comfortable in his bare feet," she said.

"And?"

"*And* your son took off his socks before I could stop him."

"Uh-oh. How did his feet look?"

She squeezed her eyes shut. "Well, he will definitely need some moss control this spring."

"Good Lord. What did you do?"

"What any mortified mother would do," she answered. "I lunged across the room and covered his feet with a magazine."

"Did the nurse look shocked?"

"I don't know. She ran out of the room when I screamed, 'Take me, Jesus!'"

I gave my wife a moment to collect herself.

"So next," she continued, "I spit in my hand and started washing his feet. But that went too slowly, so I hoisted him on the counter, put his feet in the sink, and gave him a sponge bath."

"That worked?" I asked.

"All but the dirty toenails. I scraped those clean with a tongue depressor."

"Did anyone catch you?"

"No, but the doctor walked in just as I was drying his feet off with gauze."

"What did he say?"

"He said that he raised three boys himself, and he knew exactly what I was going through."

I smiled with relief. "So then why did you say we needed to switch pediatricians?"

"Because," she replied, "I haven't got to the underwear part yet."

I have given the mystery of God's plan an exorbitant amount of thought (hence, a book). So has my sister, especially after one fateful trip several years ago to toddler gym with her boys.

I caught wind of the incident when my mother phoned to tell me she was at the gym with my sister and nephews. Apparently, during class, my sister left her boys with my mom and went to the restroom. When she returned, she unknowingly had a toilet-seat cover hanging out of her pants like a tail.

I can't prove it, but I'm pretty sure God saw this too before my sister hopped on the trampoline. And every time my sister shot into the air, the toilet-seat cover fluttered like a wind sock.

"Up and down, up and down she went," my mom later explained ... laughing. My sister even did some twists and spins.

Of course, my mother claims she didn't know what was going on until she heard another parent tell her son: "Johnny, it's not nice to point!"

Why my sister didn't feel or hear the toilet-seat cover ruffling behind her, I'm not sure, because my mom said air rushing through the tear-out hole made a whistling sound.

My nephew Drew got a kick out of it. He stood by the trampoline shouting, "Look, Grandma, Mommy's got wings. She's like a butterfly."

That's when my mom called me to recommend that I write a story about the incident. I'm certain my mother could have stopped my sister before she climbed on the trampoline. But then again, I'm pretty sure my mom didn't need to call me either.

Of course, the real question is, "What is God's plan in my sister's humiliation?" In Proverbs 3:5–6 are the words "Trust in the LORD with all your heart and lean not on your own understanding; in all your ways submit to him, and he will make your paths straight."

That's not altogether comforting when all the other kids in the gym class start begging their mommies for butterfly wings too.

The apostle Paul wrote, "Not only so, but we also glory in our sufferings, because we know that suffering produces perseverance; perseverance, character; and character, hope. And hope does not put us to shame, because God's love has been poured out into our hearts through the Holy Spirit, who has been given to us" (Rom. 5:3–5).

I understand the sentiment. And I believe Paul's sincerity when he wrote it, but these words are difficult to swallow when you open your front door to find a complete stranger standing on your stoop with a scowl while holding your child, who you were pretty sure was supposed to be inside the house.

Want to feel imperfect and alone? Discover that your child was in mortal danger and you didn't even know it. Now that's humiliating.

In our defense, we had a dead-bolt lock on our front door to prevent the children from escaping outdoors undetected. My son was eighteen months older than his sister and famous for getting into things and places he was told not to be. Since we knew we had a curious child, we bought all the modern gizmos designed to protect from hazards.

The lock on the door served us well. Unfortunately, my son developed a step faster than my wife and I were prepared for (and we still don't have that timing down, four kids later). One day, while I was at work (my alibi), my wife was folding laundry in the bedroom when our son, then three, turned the key in the dead bolt. He opened the door, and his eighteen-month-old sister walked outside. A few moments later, there was the knock. When my wife opened the door, she discovered a woman holding our daughter in her arms.

"She was in the street," the lady said, indignantly. "Hmmph."

Needless to say, my wife was mortified, in tears, and quite possibly ready to hand over her children to the authorities. She called and begged me to come home. "I can't be trusted—I'm a horrible parent," she confessed. "Hurry ... and bring a hammer and nails to seal the door."

It took days to console her. Just as she started to feel better, my sister called to rub salt in the wound. Apparently, she knew the lady who had discovered our daughter, and she heard all about what awful parents we were. Let's just say the tone in her voice wasn't much better than the tone of the driver who had found our daughter.

Now, fast-forward a few years. *The same thing happened to my sister.* She was upstairs when she heard her five-year-old crying downstairs. Minutes before, she had listened to her husband and son discussing something that made her son upset. As her husband left for work, her child was still crying, and my sister-in-law chalked it up to a typical morning. Seconds later, she realized something wasn't right. She rushed downstairs to find that her sobbing son was actually outside, alone. Somehow, he'd gotten locked out of the house.

As she opened the front door to let her son in, she spotted a neighbor across the street standing outside with his arms crossed, staring at her with an indignant expression.

I'd like to say that what comes around goes around, but I'd only be telling you that to ease the guilt my wife and I felt when it happened to us. Okay, maybe I did enjoy my sister's lesson just a little bit, but of course that is just another fine example of my imperfections.

Sigh.

REFLECTION

For as long as there have been frustrations, pain, and even suffering, human beings have looked toward the heavens to ask God, who is all-powerful and merciful, why He would allow these things to happen to us. Even now, two thousand years after Jesus came to shed more divine light on the matter, we are *still* wondering about God's plan and why He gave our children free will to do the things they do.

More thoughtful and holy thinkers than me (an understatement) have tackled the question, and the takeaway is this: it's a mystery, mostly, but in its raw form, these parental mishaps help us get closer to God.

God doesn't text us, nor does He friend us on Facebook, so to remind us He's there, He does things like inspire our three-year-old to run down the street … naked … again.

Parental mishaps help us get closer to God.

Another way to describe it is that every good story from literature has a conflict. It's a rule: no conflict, no story. It's part of our nature to be drawn to the struggle. And we experience personal and spiritual growth only when we are challenged to do so through, yes, conflict. The same is true with God. We often get closer to His grace and mercy during the times that make us throw our hands up to the sky and scream, "Why me, Lord?"

In no way am I comparing my wife's trip to the pediatrician, or my sister's visit to the gym, to the challenges Helen Keller faced, but she did say, "I thank God for my handicaps, for through them I have found myself, my work, and my God." If she can do it, certainly my sister can remove her toilet-seat cover and do the same.

When everything is going smoothly, most of us forget to talk to God—so He nudges us. But rest assured, He's on our side. And yes, He agrees that the kids should chew with their mouths closed. Just saying.

Verse: "And the God of all grace, who called you to his eternal glory in Christ, after you have suffered a little while, will himself restore you and make you strong, firm and steadfast. To him be the power for ever and ever. Amen" (1 Pet. 5:10–11).

Further Reading:

> Psalm 34
> Isaiah 42
> James 1

Prayer: There may not be any better truth for me today than Isaiah 41:10, "So do not fear, for I am with you; do not be dismayed, for I am your God. I will strengthen you and help you; I will uphold you with my righteous right hand." Lord, let those words sink in for me, and bring them to my lips as many times as I need them today. I know You love me. I will honor You with my trust. Amen.

CHAPTER TWO

Why Did God Give My Kids Free Will?

If I had a dollar for every time my kids argued and fought … I could've afforded my own apartment.

When they were young, they bickered, cried, brawled—and that was on a good day.

"Dad!" Jack once cried from upstairs. "Michael fed my baseball card to the dog!"

I waited for a moment to see if the storm would blow over.

"Dad!"

Sighing, I marched up the stairs.

"Michael," I said in a stern voice as I walked into the playroom, pointing to the shreds of drool-covered paper littered on the floor, "this is not acceptable. You are going to buy Jack a new baseball card with your own money."

"Wh-what—*why?*" my son whined. *"No fair!* Jack fed the dog the cape off my Batman toy!"

I exhaled loudly. It was immediately obvious that this was not going to be a cut-and-dried case. It was also evident that the dog probably needed a laxative.

I'm sure God has His reasons for giving us free will, but can't that start for kids after they graduate and move out?

There are some sound reasons to deny children any dominion. For example, think how better prepared they'd be if free will came, say, on their twenty-fifth birthday. They'd have all those years of forming great habits by dutifully following God's commandments to a T. As adults, they'd make far fewer mistakes. Their adulthood would be far more enriching.

And their parents would benefit too.

Case in point: Every year when my boy's birthday came around, he begged to have a slumber party. Every year, my wife nodded yes—and then wept in the broom closet. Simultaneously, I went into the garage and painted large signs that read: "You Break, You Buy!"

When it came right down to it, having one preteen in the house was grounds for parental insanity. Inviting four more to our home …? That bordered on criminal intent.

Boys are gross, ill-mannered, loud, and destructive. And they know this.

But as long as other parents were having overnight parties for their children and insisting on inviting my son, I was forced to do the same. So each year, before there was anything I could do to stop it, each child's parent stood on my porch, pushed their son inside the door, and repeated the standard line we all learned in PTA: "Call me if my son is any trouble."

Then, they'd run to their cars, unplug their cell phones, and buy one-way tickets to Bermuda.

Or so it felt as I stood there, waving goodbye to the last car, as five boys slid down the stairs on the good sofa cushions and into my bad knee.

I turned and ordered them into the kitchen for dinner.

I, however, made the mistake of hesitating, and as I hobbled slowly into the kitchen, the food was completely gone.

I stared blankly at the empty pizza boxes. "Did they stuff them in their pockets?" I asked my wife, who, incidentally, had had a slice actually in her hand, but when she blinked, someone stole her toppings.

Suddenly, a loud, obnoxious burp resonated from the table. "That's burp code," some obnoxious kid announced. "It means we're thirsty."

I walked over with soda pop and filled each of their cups.

I stood staring for a moment.

"What's wrong?" someone asked.

"Well," I began, "when I was a kid, if we didn't say '*thank you*,' our drinks were taken away."

Another kid belched. "That's burp code for 'thank you.'"

The children finished what they didn't spill on the table and floor and then headed back upstairs to play, which mostly meant throwing plastic toys at one another until someone started to bleed.

Occasionally, I swept through the house noting the damage. Later, I walked into the living room and asked my wife, "Who is the redheaded kid?"

"That's Richard. Why?"

"Because I caught him jumping on our bed with a can of orange pop in his hands."

Her eyes went wide. "Did you tell him to stop?"

"No, I asked if he needed pretzels," I answered. "Of course I told him to stop."

"What did he say?"

"He said we were really cool parents because we have orange dots on our ceiling. He said his mom and dad only bought a white ceiling."

My wife's face sank. "You know, next year, I think that you need to make bigger warning signs."

"No way," I retorted, sitting down next to her. "Next year, I'm printing on the invitations: 'All children must be accompanied by an adult.'"

And then there was my favorite activity: trying to shepherd children with free will out the front door within a specified time frame. I liked that game almost as much as jamming my finger in a sliding door.

The challenge, of course, was leaving the house in the morning before there was no longer a reason to leave—like, say, because it was nighttime.

There were many reasons I recall having a problem ushering children from point A to point B. For starters, when my kids heard me shout, "It's time to go," they had the sudden urge to do something else, such as use the bathroom, call a friend, or run next door to have waffles with the neighbors. Once, as I backed my car out of the garage, a child got stuck up a tree.

I wonder what they were thinking when they heard me announce our impending departure.

Hmm, Dad said it's time to go. I'd better hurry and set up the Monopoly game—there's not much time to play. They always had some excuse to procrastinate.

Meanwhile, I would stand by the door, talking to the cat. "Didn't I just tell everyone it was time to leave?"

Cats don't care.

Missing items of clothing also played a huge role in delaying a departure—namely, shoes and coats. They were never where they needed to be when it was time to go … like on the children.

One time, as the school bus was parked at the curb, my son announced his shoe was missing.

"Again?" I asked. I ran frantically around the house, shouting questions. "Have you checked under the couch?"

"Yes."

"By the computer?"

"Yes."

"In the mailbox?" (That's where we found his socks.)

He assured me he had no idea *who* would have taken his shoe.

I said, "Probably someone trying to drive your dad insane." He laughed and then went to school in slippers. Later, his shoe showed up in his closet. Who would have guessed it?

I'd like to say the children did these things only when they didn't want to go somewhere, but this was not the case. Even going to the movies or an amusement park could be a challenge. The kids would get so excited they'd lose all control of their good sense and run around in circles, bounce on the couches, or crack the whip, sending the youngest into a wall. Instead of leaving on time, we'd wait while someone went looking for a Band-Aid.

Nonetheless, I did, however, get better at organizing the children. I no longer waited until it was time to go to get them motivated. I learned to give everyone plenty of warning.

"Kids, we're going to Grandma's house for Thanksgiving. I want you ready to go with your shoes and jacket on your bodies by six o'clock."

"Okay, Dad, but can we finish trick-or-treating first?"

Even so, I just knew one of the kids would show up to Thanksgiving in flip-flops.

Free will is tough on getting chores done too. More precisely, it's brutal for the person *supervising* the chores.

Do you want to know the difference between me overseeing my children doing yard work and prison guards supervising convicts working the chain gang? Prison guards are armed.

I, on the other hand, had only my yelling voice (and what was left of my sanity) to protect me.

I relished the opportunity to teach my children the value of an honest day's work. And they, of course, relished the opportunity to take me down to my knees.

Each summer started the same way. Roughly three days before school was out, I would make a big speech about the family pulling together to keep the yard looking nice for the neighborhood to enjoy. I'd say things like "A family that weeds together, eats together" and "I don't want to see anyone kicking the tops of the weeds off this year."

It may shock you, but my children could not care less if their mom and I, the neighbors, or anyone else enjoyed our yard in the summer. In fact, my son once wanted to send a flyer around the block announcing that the Swarners were going "environmental" that year and would be letting nature take its course. He drew a picture of our house with brown grass and weeds large enough to shade small woodland animals.

Without their buy-in, I tended to play the role of grumpy foreman. As a child, my oldest son, who is now married and with a son of his own, needed constant supervision. I was forever sticking my head out the back door yelling, "Get back to work!"

"I am," he'd argue.

"You are? I can see you suntanning on the roof of the shed, you know. It might be easier to pull the weeds if you were closer to the ground."

My daughter was the opposite. She just cried. She also said I was unfair to make her weed. "My friends don't have to pull weeds!"

"That's true," I told her. "That would be weird if I made your friends pull our weeds."

When she did get to work, our conversations often went like this:

> Daughter: Dad, I'm done weeding my area.
> Me: (inspecting) What about that weed?
> Daughter: What weed? I don't see any weeds. Where do you see a weed?
> Me: (pointing) There ... blocking the window.

My youngest two were a bigger challenge. I was lucky if I could keep them on task for five minutes. I'd send them out to do a quick and easy weeding job, and a half hour later, one would walk into the house with a gob of doggy doo-doo on a stick. "Look what I found, Dad. I think the dog ate a dish towel."

I suppose I would've liked my children to have had the experience of pulling together as a family for a common goal. I wanted them to know that being part of a group requires everyone doing their fair share.

At least, that's what I told my children when I found them in the backyard sitting in lawn chairs with a box of frozen treats and ten of the little neighborhood kids weeding our rose beds.

> Son: But, Dad, they want to do our work in exchange for Otter Pops.

I decided to hire a landscaper.

Speaking of the neighborhood kids, I used to wish God hadn't given them free will either. I suppose that every street across this great country has a kid like Peter, the first grader who lived down the road from me.

You know the type. The sort of child who, for whatever reason, has no boundaries. Where, on any given day, he'll ride his bike across your front lawn, enter your house as if it were his own, open your refrigerator without permission, and ask, "Got anything to drink?"

It's not that I had anything against the boy. He was bright, clever, funny—a nice kid. It was just hard to appreciate those qualities when he opened my shower and asked when I would be getting out.

Quite frankly, it was difficult to let your guard down when Peter was roaming the neighborhood. Once, I made the mistake of stretching out a blanket in the backyard and taking a nap. I woke an hour later, eyeball to eyeball with the kid.

"Gee, Mr. Swarner, I put five ants up your nose, and you didn't wake up once. I wonder when they'll come back out."

The list of examples feels endless.

Now, the biggest dilemma for an adult like me, one who didn't want his nickname around the neighborhood to be Mean Old Mr. Swarner, was finding gentle and kind ways to tell Peter (who rarely understood subtle hints) to go home. After all, there's nothing worse than hurting a little child's feelings ... unless, of course, he's telling you that you're his best friend *as* you are hurting his feelings.

So, after a couple of hours of dealing with Peter, I'd start searching for polite ways to encourage him to find somewhere else to play. I'd say something like "Gosh, isn't it lunchtime?" Or "You must be getting tired of hanging out with me." Or "Run, Peter—zombies!"

One time, I even tried a classic approach. When Peter wasn't looking, I turned my head and, in a high-pitched voice, called his name as if I were his mother. He didn't fall for it, but his dog ran up and licked my face.

Finally, I was too exhausted. I just wanted to have a quiet night at home. So when Peter knocked at our kitchen window, I whispered loudly to my family as we ate dinner around the table. "Shhhh. Everyone, freeze. Don't say a word. Maybe he'll go away."

"He can see us, Dad," my son announced. "His face is smashed against the window."

"Well, then pretend you're dead," I said.

"Sitting up?"

"No. One by one, everyone fall off your chairs."

As we lay there, Peter walked around to the front door, came inside, and asked if he could play too.

"At my house, we never get to pretend that we've died of food poisoning!" he exclaimed. "You guys are really cool. I'm coming by more often."

REFLECTION

As I have pondered free will, I've had to admit that my troubles with it are the same as how I feel about the other struggles in my life. Namely, I strain to trust the process. To say God shouldn't have given children free will is to say I don't *trust* God. God believes in my kids, as I should understand He believes in me.

In John 15:16 we are told, "You did not choose me, but I chose you." That should be the beginning and the end of the story, or as my mother fondly liked to say, "Because I told you so."

And yet …

It's not any easier to watch the wear and tear of free will in my children (especially when it requires paying to fix broken windows or seeing the hurt in their eyes) than it is to witness my own consequences with free will. It's not a simple thing to be human. The freedom to choose what we think, do, and say has its highs and lows.

In the end, though, we are blessed with free will because it's one more way to know we are loved by our God. We are created to make wise decisions in line with His Word—as well as, I believe, to learn from our sins and see that we are still loved by Him when we miss the mark.

Our children are doubly blessed. They can know God's unconditional love, *and* they can feel blessed by our trust and love for them too, even when they fail. We can honor our Lord by honoring and trusting His (and our) children.

> Our children are doubly blessed. They can know God's unconditional love, *and* they can feel blessed by our trust and love for them too, even when they fail.

God knows kids won't always use their free will to proper ends. It helps to remember that, especially when your son blows the paper off his drink straw in the restaurant and it accidentally lands in the face of an elderly woman in the next booth. I can assure you that God isn't trying to mess with you. It just feels that way.

Verse: "And if it seem evil unto you to serve the LORD, choose you this day whom ye will serve; whether the gods which your fathers served that were on the other side of the flood, or the gods of the

Amorites, in whose land ye dwell: but as for me and my house, we will serve the LORD" (Josh. 24:15 KJV).

Further Reading:

> Proverbs 16
> Galatians 5:13
> Revelation 3

Prayer: Lord, in the haze of my daily triumphs and tribulations, I pause today to thank You for the choice You gave me to follow You. I am strengthened by my decision to love You, and I am emboldened to seek Your guidance and compassion in good times and bad. Amen.

CHAPTER THREE

Honor Thy Father

I long considered posting the Ten Commandments in my children's rooms. And underlining number five ... a dozen times.

I would've liked to start with them honoring me by not touching the tape, batteries, toilet paper, or glitter in the house. That would've been a tall order.

I was talking with my friend John, and I discovered that I wasn't the only dad who could never find a lick of tape in the house when it's needed. Like me, John had kids who were in a perpetual state of fastening things together. Bedsheets made into living room tents, Happy Meal toys that needed mending, little sisters strapped to trees.

My children were tape maniacs.

You name it: Scotch, masking, electrical, duct, medical. Just empty spools littered around the house.

And I usually discovered we were out when I was in the middle of a building project, standing on a ladder, holding two loose wires together, shouting, "I need more tape ... and someone please turn off the power! Ow!"

In a pinch, I had to resort to other means to bind objects together, such as glue, paper clips, string, and even hair spray. Once, I wrapped a birthday gift with bungee cords.

I'm not exactly sure why my children voraciously consumed tape, but I had my suspicions. I wouldn't be surprised if our nation's tape manufacturers were running commercials on TikTok, teaching our children how to use huge amounts of tape when we're at work so we have to keep buying more. Where else could they have learned to use an entire roll to rig a sled behind their bikes?

Several years back, for example, I had a gift to wrap for my wife's birthday. "*Where's the Scotch tape?*" I shouted.

"I used it all," my daughter announced. "Barbie's head snapped off. See?"

I examined the inch-thick band of tape around the doll's neck. "Did you need to use this much?"

"Yes," she responded. "I'm pretending it's a neck brace. Malibu Ken rear-ended Barbie's car. She's pressing charges."

Next, I rummaged through the hall closet. "*Where's all the masking tape?*"

"We used it to make a fort in the kitchen," my son explained. "But Mom made us take it down."

I blew a sigh of relief. "Good, so bring me the tape you used."

"I can't," he replied.

"Why?"

"Because we rolled it into a ball and played soccer in the backyard."

"So where's the tape now?" I asked.

"Stuck to the chimney."

Finally, I looked for the duct tape. It was missing too. I sat there staring dumbly at the wrapping paper. *"Does anyone care that Dad is losing his mind?"*

My son assured me that he was concerned. "You could always use what I use when I can't find any tape," he offered.

I looked up. "What's that?"

"Spit."

I decided to go look for bungee cords.

Anyway, I gave my neighbor a case of tape and asked him to keep it safe for me until I needed it. He said he hadn't seen tape in twelve years. I think I'll call *60 Minutes*. They normally like to report on conspiracies like this.

While they're at it, they could look into the other great mystery of my life—missing batteries.

My wife and kids left me at the house for a couple of hours once, so you can imagine what I did. I enjoyed the peace and quiet. Excited, I popped some popcorn, sat on the couch, grabbed the remote control, pressed the power button for the TV, and … nothing happened.

1:00 p.m.: I remove the back from the remote control and discover that the batteries are missing. Sagging my shoulders, I stand up and start an epic search.

1:03 p.m.: The hunt begins in my teenager's room. Digging through several layers of clothes on his floor, I discover my toenail clippers, house key, tire jack, barbecue tongs, and one black dress shoe. But no sign of the batteries.

1:15 p.m.: Reaching under my daughter's bed, I shout for joy when my fingers touch something small, cold, and cylinder … only I can't seem to move it. Low-crawling under the bed, I discover I'm grasping a stale Tootsie Roll stuck to the carpet.

1:16 p.m.: I bang my head on the sideboard.

1:18 p.m.: Figuring my youngest probably stole the batteries for his electronics, I search the devices in his room for my double-A batteries, but first I have to scour the garage for the tiny little screwdriver to remove the screws holding in the batteries on the various devices. The screwdriver is missing too. I look to the heavens and question God's infinite wisdom in choosing me to be a father. Then, I find a crusty black banana peel in my toolbox.

1:25 p.m.: I ask the dog, "Where are the batteries, boy?"

1:26 p.m.: I realize I'm starting to lose it.

1:30 p.m.: I find the mother lode. In my son's bottom desk drawer, there are forty-seven double-A batteries. Delighted, I grab two, run joyously to the family room, sit back down on my couch, blow out a satisfied breath of air, pop the batteries into the remote control, point the device at the TV, and … nothing happens. The batteries are dead.

1:45 p.m.: After tearing a magazine into small pieces, I feel better, and I trudge back and forth from my son's room, unsuccessfully trying all the batteries from his desk drawer in the remote control until I finally collapse to the floor and have a hissy fit.

2:13 p.m.: Taking in a deep breath, I pick myself up and continue the search.

2:15 p.m.: Inspecting the playroom, I find various other electronic toys, but the backs are completely missing ... as are any batteries.

2:34 p.m.: I sit on the stairs feeling sorry for myself and mumbling, "I just wanted to relax with my remote control and watch TV. That's all I asked for. Why is this happening to me?"

3:05 p.m.: My wife walks into the house and catches me stealing the batteries from her portable hand mixer. She crosses her arms and exclaims, "So you're the one who took the batteries out of the remote control?"

I would have been better off taking a nap.

Now, I don't want to give you the willies, but we went through a lot of toilet paper in my house too.

And I don't know why. With all puns aside, we didn't eat that much bran.

I was certain, however, that it was the children who were the problem. I'm not sure if they were selling the TP to their friends, burying it, or writing their school reports on it.

Frankly, I wish I had a roll of TP for every time I saw that sad, lonely, empty cardboard tube on the holder fluttering its last flake of Charmin over the heat vent.

My kids were never too keen on replacing the roll. I suppose it was too much out of their day to take off the plastic roller, remove the old tube, and put on a new roll. If they'd had time to do that, I guess they'd also have had time to hang their coats on the rack and chew their food.

I often wondered what they were thinking when they ripped that last shred of the paper off the spindle.

> Child 1: That's good enough.
> Child 2: No one can prove I was here last.

But this didn't explain why in my house we were often at the crisis point—a complete wiping out of the TP. It wasn't just a matter of rooting under the bathroom sink for a new roll because the kids hadn't replaced the TP—it was that there was nothing under the sink to fetch.

Unfortunately, I didn't always know this was the case until it was too late … and there were guests in the living room … and I'd have to shout through the crack under the bathroom door: "Hello? Uh, would someone please get my wife?"

And it wasn't like I hadn't had this discussion with my children.

"Kids," I said, "are you eating the toilet paper?"

I've even organized a few TP classes for them.

Me: Today, children, we will run through a couple of key toilet-paper drills. All right, you can stand back up and stop giggling now. The first drill includes the three-step process I like to call "replacing the toilet paper so Dad knows you love him." Our second drill is a bit tougher. It deals with using the last roll of TP. I like to call it "how to write a shopping list."

Of course, there's always a smart-mouth in the group.

Child: You can't prove that we are the ones using the last roll, you know.
Me: True. But how come I never hear you cussing from the bathroom?

Out of desperation, I finally consulted an expert in the matter—my mother. I asked her how she managed to raise children with enough courtesy and respect to keep the TP spindle refreshed at all times.

Tea came out of her nose she laughed so hard. "You think you replaced the TP in our house?" she said. "Your father and I were ready to build an outhouse in the backyard for you kids, but the zoning laws wouldn't allow it."

"So, there's no hope?" I asked.

"Not without a waiver from the mayor."

And speaking of the bathroom, why are children so fascinated with a plugged-up toilet?

When the commode got blocked at my house, the kids acted as if they were staring at a winning lottery ticket.

> Child 1: I can't believe it—it's finally happened!
> The toilet is plugged!
> Child 2: Pinch me—I'm dreaming!

It was usually shortly after this discovery that the giggling started. What at first were children pointing and laughing at a swirling pot soon turned into crazed kids screaming with joy as the water spilled over the rim. You'd think they were tourists at Niagara Falls.

"Hurry, grab the camera!"

It was like they'd been waiting their entire year to see an actual toilet overflow.

"This is just how I pictured it. Uh-oh—run!"

They also couldn't wait to share the news, and they could barely get the words out.

"Dad, the (*ha-ha*) toilet is (holding his stomach and falling into hysterics) is ... is ... I ... can't ... breathe ..."

"What's going on?" I asked the other child, whose face was beet red and who was struggling to get any audible word out of his mouth.

"T-t-t ..." He joined his brother chortling on the floor.

I usually got to the bottom of things, however, when I'd hear my wife moaning from upstairs. *"Ken! The toilet is overflowing!"*

To which I would shout back, "Well, that certainly explains why the children are slobbering all over themselves."

Once, as I stood up, the kids excitedly sprang to their feet. "Are you going to get the plunger, Dad?"

I blinked. "No, I thought I'd go grab my surfboard and catch a wave down the stairs. Of course I'm going to go get the plunger."

Then, as if the whole neighborhood needed to be in on the action, the children screamed, *"He's going to get the plunger!"*

A plunger is a big deal to kids. It's mysterious. It's hilarious. It's gross.

A few minutes later, I walked into the house with the infamous tool slung over my shoulder. I passed the children, who were lined up in the hallway, pointing with excitement as if I were a Macy's Thanksgiving Day Parade float.

> Parade Announcer 1: Here comes the Ken Swarner
> float. Nice plunger this year.
> Parade Announcer 2: (giggling uncontrollably) Go
> to commercial! Coffee is coming out of my nose!

When I finally reached the bathroom, the children stood in the hallway saying things like "Sick," "Disgusting," and "Gross." This was part of their overall celebration.

I gave them a sideways glance.

"Dad, how can you do that? Aren't you weirded out?"

"Not at all," I replied sarcastically. "This is why I became a dad. I wish this happened more often."

Later, as I washed the plunger off in the sink, I heard one of them whisper: "I don't think I'll ever brush my teeth in here again."

Finally, I gave my usual lecture about using less toilet paper, and then I returned the plunger to the garage.

Later that night, I overheard my son saying his prayers. "God, thanks for making our toilet overflow today. That was great. Would it be a sin if I were to use my stuffed dinosaur to plug it up next week?"

I knew then I'd better say my own prayers.

And then there was glitter.

In 2013, the Swarners bought a $2.35 bottle of glitter. That was our first mistake.

Opening it … that was our second.

The children made all sorts of craft projects with the glitter and, along the way, managed to spill about half of the bottle throughout the house.

Now, if you have been through this, you know how well glitter can hide deep down in the carpet and in corners, immune to routine vacuuming and sweeping. And you also know how sticky glitter can be, so that when no one is looking and from out of nowhere, it jumps like fleas on a dog.

So, for years, I found this stuff popping up in all sorts of unexpected places—the bottom of my son's dirty socks, the cat's fur, the clothes hamper, even in my briefcase. Worse, however, were the number of times the specks of glitter adhered to my face. I never knew how they got there, but roughly once a month, I would walk into an important business meeting with, unbeknownst to me, my face twinkling like a disco ball.

One year, my coworkers started singing Bee Gees' tunes when I strolled in the door. Doris Greenberg in purchasing once moon-walked past me on her way to the coffee machine.

Of course, everyone had a great laugh at my expense. Even Fred Dorchester from accounting enjoyed it—until his daughter brought home some glitter from school. The next day, Fred attended his monthly poker game glistening around the eyes.

I finally announced to my family that it was time to purge the Swarner home of all glitter ... even if I had to tear the house down to the foundation.

First, I went over *everything* with a deluxe, mondo-suction industrial vacuum. I spent hours running the machine throughout our rooms, sucking the heck out of everything. The bad news, of course, was that it didn't pick up much of the sticky glitter. The good news was that, according to our vet, the cat's hair would eventually grow back.

Next, I tried a different tactic. I ordered everyone to take the clothes, bed linens, and cushions outside and beat the glitter out of them with brooms. Unfortunately, the spectacle not only created a plume of glitter so that our yard was now infested like the inside, but we also made our community newspaper, under the headline "Are These People Nuts?"

Needless to say, the glitter remained. However, I can report that my wife didn't see the cleaning operation as a complete disaster.

As I sat exhausted in a chair, she shouted at me, "Hold it—don't move!"

Startled, I asked, "Why?"

"Because I want to get my camera and take a picture of you," she exclaimed, rushing over to the kitchen counter.

I groaned. "So we can remember the Great Glitter Hunt?"

"No," she said, snapping my picture. "Because you've got glitter all over your face again."

"So what's new?"

"Well, you look like one of Santa's elves. It will make a good picture for our family Christmas card: 'Jingles Swarner wishes you a Merry Christmas.' Can you stand up and look jolly for a minute?"

REFLECTION 1

Researchers from Switzerland made a startling discovery in the 1990s when they examined whether a parent's church habits affected their offsprings' choices as adults: they found that fathers are the determining factor.[1]

Here are the stats: If mom goes to church regularly but dad attends only every so often, only 3.4 percent of children in that environment will grow up to be regular churchgoers. That number slips to 1.5 percent if dad never goes to church. If mom and dad attend church regularly together, however, the number dramatically increases to 33 percent. Now, get this: if dad attends church regularly but mom goes only every so often, the results rise further to 38 percent. Amazing, right? That is not the end, however. If dad goes to church all the time but mom *never* goes, 44 percent of kids will grow up to become regular churchgoers.

Dad, the pressure is on you!

When my two oldest were in high school, I gave in to their complaints about attending church. I didn't make them go—and today, neither attends church. I regret that decision, because maybe that contributed to their absence from church today. I since mended my ways with the two youngest. We went to church nearly every Sunday, and often I could be heard shouting up the stairs to "Get a move on" and "No, you can't wear a tank top to church!"

I get it. Moms often become white noise to their kids. They work diligently in all aspects of their children's upbringing to be good, moral people. Dads don't chime in as much. So when we do, the kids take more notice. It is our responsibility as Christian fathers to get our family to church.

REFLECTION 2

Thinking back on the stories in this chapter, a thought occurred to me. God is *my* Father ... so in what ways do I frustrate Him? My constant lack of faith maybe? The times I know the right way and yet make the wrong decision?

I can get irritated with my kids about missing batteries, but maybe I see a little too much of myself in them. I know I fall short in honoring my holy Father as I should. The frustrations I have with my children should be a reminder for myself to shape up. Maybe that's the message God has been trying to send all along.

The frustrations I have with my

children should be a reminder

for myself to shape up. Maybe

that's the message God has

been trying to send all along.

REFLECTION 3

I should also note at this point in the book that I wallpapered the kids' bathroom with the following from Proverbs: "Listen, my son, to your father's instruction and do not forsake your mother's teaching. They are a garland to grace your head and a chain to adorn your neck" (Prov. 1:8–9).

Verse: "Children, obey your parents in the Lord, for this is right. 'Honor your father and mother'—which is the first commandment with a promise—'so that it may go well with you and that you may enjoy long life on the earth.' Fathers, do not exasperate your children; instead, bring them up in the training and instruction of the Lord" (Eph. 6:1–4).

Further Reading:

> Proverbs 4:1–9
> Luke 15:11–32
> John 8

Prayer: I come to You, Lord, humbled by the gift of my children, awed by the choices in front of me, encouraged to guide them in Your light. Bestow upon me the courage to speak Your truth to them. Provide the compassion and patience I will need to lead them, as well as the perseverance to fulfill my duties as Your disciple. Amen.

CHAPTER FOUR

Honor Thy Mother

I think the children may have driven my wife to the brink of insanity.

Once, in the middle of the day, I saw her wearing her nightgown and dashing from the kitchen, cradling a piece of chocolate cake, and mumbling, "My precious." I'm no expert, but even I started to think something was amiss.

So, like any caring spouse would do, I asked her, *"What are you doing?"*

She froze. "What do you mean?"

"I mean, why are you running upstairs with that piece of chocolate cake?"

"It's the last one," she answered, holding it behind her back.

"And?"

She grinned devilishly. "And the children aren't getting it."

I sat down on the step. "Honey, why the sudden need to hide baked goods?"

"Because," she answered, "there will come a day, very soon, when the air will be chilly outside, and I will feel like lighting a fire in the fireplace. I'll pour myself a hot cup of tea and curl up on the couch with the cat and a good book. Then it will suddenly occur to me: *Chocolate cake would hit the spot.* But unlike yesterday, when this very scenario indeed transpired, I won't walk to the counter and lift the cake box only to stare at a couple crumbs and the lick marks where the kids ran their tongues across the empty plate. No!" she cried, the mania returning to her eyes. "I'll *get* my cake!"

"How?"

She held out the plate. "I'm making a deposit in the cake bank. Before it's too late."

"Really?" I asked. "What did the children say about that?"

"They said they wanted a bite."

"What did you say?"

"I said, 'Give me my fork back!'"

"So where are you going to hide the cake?"

She gave me the evil eye. "Wouldn't you like to know."

I blanched. "Isn't this secrecy a little rash?"

She shook her head. "This cake," she explained, lifting it high into the air, "is all that exists in this world that I can still call my own."

I paused for a moment. "So, sweetie, you're saying that eventually you're going to scurry off somewhere in the house and eat that piece of cake like a common mouse?"

"Of course not," she fired back. "I'll get a glass of milk first."

I suppose I should have seen this coming. For years, my wife had complained about how her once perfectly ordered world, where she could count on something being there when she wanted it, had crumbled before her eyes.

I left her there on the steps so I could go find the family medical book.

A little while later, I found my son sitting on the stairs … eating the piece of chocolate cake.

"What are you doing?" I asked him, searching for my wife. "Where did you get that cake?"

He shrugged. "Someone left it on the banister."

"Where's Mom?"

"I don't know. She was in the attic, but then I heard her say something about going downstairs to find Saran wrap."

"Son," I said, sitting next to him and putting my arm around his shoulder, "can I give you some fatherly advice?"

He nodded.

"Run!"

The children's memorabilia filled two closets in our house, covered the sawhorse in the garage, jammed a utility cupboard, and if something wasn't done soon, were destined next for my side of the bed.

Therefore, I announced at the dinner table that it was time to consolidate the art projects, awards, holiday cards, grades, and other mementos our sons and daughter had brought home since preschool, into one central, confined location. "Preferably Grandma's house," I said.

Since my wife balked at that idea, and because our housing covenants don't allow silos, she agreed to go through the stuff and weed it down until everything fit into four large plastic bins.

After a few hours of effort, she called the children and me into the room.

"How's it going?" I asked.

"What I want to keep won't all fit into the bins," she said in frustration. "In this pile, I have the ones I want, and in this other pile," she said, pointing to a stack of three things—a tiny slip of paper, an old lunch box, and a broken toothpick house—"are what I'm willing to throw out."

I put my arm around her. "So you need someone to make an unbiased decision of what must go?"

"No," she said, looking at me in alarm. "I need larger bins."

I rummaged around in the "keep" stack. "Well, honey, this can certainly go."

"Wait!" she shouted, snatching the paper away from me. She studied it for a few moments. "Ken, we can't throw that out."

"You want to save our son's spelling test?"

"Of course, it's precious," she replied.

"He got a D-minus."

"I know," she said, pointing at the sheet. "But look at the nice thing the teacher wrote on it."

I studied the paper. "It says, 'Nice improvement.'"

"See?" she said, carefully placing it in the bin.

Michael poked his head over the large pile. "What about this?"

My wife's face broke out into a silly grin. "Oh, I don't think I can really let that one go." She held to her heart the macaroni necklace our daughter had made in kindergarten. "I wore this to the country club dinner/dance."

"You went into public with it?" my daughter said in disgust.

"Of course I did—you asked me to." She turned to me. "Remember what the waiter said?"

"No."

She smiled giddily at the children. "He said the pasta really brought out my eyes."

Our daughter grabbed the necklace. "Hey! Why do four of the noodles look cooked?"

My wife frowned. "They dipped in my soup."

We went back and forth over 125 more things, each one landing back in the keep pile until I finally gave up. "Why don't you put everything back where it was—it's obvious you aren't ready for this. I suppose I could always sleep on the couch."

"I can keep all of it?" she asked.

"Yes."

She held up the tiny slip of paper in the discard pile. "Even Jack's first bicycle lock combination?"

I nodded.

"Oh, thank you," she exclaimed, hugging me. "You're the best."

I've been kicking myself ever since. I could have given her that for Valentine's Day.

Mothers love such memories and, equally, the special times they spend with their children. One Christmas, my wife suggested that our daughter make cross-stitch tea towels as gifts for the grandmas.

"I'll teach you how to do it," my wife said excitedly.

I was in the room when she made this announcement. My first thought was *The grandmas will love hand-embroidered tea towels for Christmas.* My second thought was *How many Irish coffees did my wife drink?*

"Okay, sweetie," my wife said with her patient voice turned on full blast. "We take the threaded needle and pull it through the fabric here."

"What? I don't get it," my daughter said anxiously.

Let's just say the two of them didn't exactly have a good track record when it came to mother-daughter projects. In the end, my daughter usually had a nice, completed craft and my wife had lost five years off her life.

"Why don't I do the first stitch so you can see how it's done?"

"No! I want to do it!"

I know what my wife was thinking when she suggested the tea towel project. She had in her mind this Norman Rockwell–like scene of the two of them sitting quietly by the light of the fire, cross-stitching gifts like pioneer moms and daughters surely did during a simpler, happier time.

What she forgot, however, was that our daughter was thinking, *What fun it will be to turn my mother's early settler fantasy into a living hell.*

"Okay, okay, you can do it yourself. Look, you need to cross-stitch the wings with this brown thread, so start right here with your needle."

"What? I don't get it!"

Our daughter sensed how important the activity was to her mother—and she wasn't about to go easy on her.

"You need to cross-stitch starting here."

"What?"

"You need to cross-stitch—"

"Huh?"

"You … need … to …"

"What?"

"Y … o … u … You … n … e …"

Before they started the holiday craft project, I asked my wife, "Are you sure you want to do this tea towel thing?"

"You don't think Claire can do it?" she responded, completely missing my point.

"Sure, she can," I replied. "But after *this* mother-daughter project is completed, it's safe to say that when I turn sixty, you're already going to be dead."

She completely ignored my warnings … again. So I settled into my favorite recliner as the two of them sat on the couch, bonding over the joyous holiday project.

"Claire, why don't you just get it over with and stab me with your needle!"

"What? Who said I'm not having fun?"

I can't say with any certainty that my daughter intentionally wanted to drive her mother insane, or that my wife is a complete masochist, but I do know that these little craft projects they did together would make a great Laurel and Hardy movie.

"Ken, you can wipe that smile off your face now!"

"Yeah, Dad!"

If my children should honor their mother, I guess that means that I should honor *my* mother too …

I'm not sure when it happened, but sometime between my childhood and now, my mom changed.

When I was a kid, I didn't have a "cool" mother. I wasn't spoiled with all the things kids wanted in the '70s and '80s. I was told that money didn't grow on trees and that if I really wanted something, I could get a job to pay for it.

Not so today!

As a grandma, my mom has long been spoiling my children with all sorts of goodies. But I didn't realize how much things had changed until the time she took my daughter shopping at the mall.

When they returned home, my then thirteen-year-old walked inside wearing the jeans my mother had just bought her. They had holes in both knees.

I said the first thing that came to my mind. "Sweetie, did you fall down?"

My daughter not only said no but also announced that the (barely) pants cost $120.

So I said the next thing that came to my mind. "Mom, did *you* fall down?"

My mother would *never* have bought me $120 jeans when I was a kid, let alone ones that conveyed the message: "Can you spare a dollar?"

I leveled this accusation at my mom. "Really, Mother? If I had asked for jeans like these, you would have thrown a hissy fit."

"That's because you were a Mr. Smarty Pants," my mom said matter-of-factly.

I turned back toward my daughter. "What else did Grandma buy you today? A thong?"

My daughter's face brightened. "How did you know?"

My mother cut me off before I could say a word. "Your daughter can't walk around with panty lines. They just aren't in style anymore, Ken."

"You never worried about me being in fashion when I was a kid," I replied. "In fact, you wanted to keep me in elastic jeans through junior high."

"They were a good deal," she fired back. "And besides, what was considered 'in style' back then wasn't appropriate."

I rolled my eyes. "But thongs and jeans torn at the knees are all the rage at the senior center?"

My mom looked at my daughter. "Your father's idea of fashion was long, stringy hair and black rock-concert T-shirts with the sleeves cut off. The neighbors were afraid to let their cats outside."

My daughter let out a small giggle.

And that's when I saw it … the truth. When I wasn't looking, my once autocratic mother had passed the parenting torch to me, while she took off in a full sprint toward the land of milk and honey, where she transformed into "cool" grandma.

I was now the fuddy-duddy parent—the disciplinarian—the one who worries about the bottom line … while my mother is cracking jokes and buying my daughter undergarments that don't show bottom lines.

Suddenly, not only did I have to reassess the mother I thought I once knew, but it was as if I had another child to watch.

"So," I said, turning back to my mom and daughter, "what's on your agenda for the rest of the day? A Chippendales concert?"

My mother turned to my daughter. "See, I told you—he's a Mr. Smarty Pants."

REFLECTION

There is an amazing bond of motherhood seen in the life of Mary, the mother of Jesus. We can learn so much from what little we know of her. She put her life on the line for God by agreeing to carry His Son, though she knew it could mean her death by stoning. It would've been completely natural for Joseph to assume she had been impregnated by another man, and he could have brought her up on charges. And yet, her faith and willingness to be God's servant overshadowed those likely consequences.

And what did she get for her trust? The opportunity to watch her beloved Son get rejected and viciously murdered.

"I am the Lord's servant.... May your word to me be fulfilled," she announced (Luke 1:38).

How did such a poor nobody get picked by God to bear His greatest gift? And where did she find the fortitude to stay faithful?

I sometimes wonder how—on a much smaller scale, of course— my wife and mom find the resilience to endure me and the kids. It can't be easy. We are often messy, ungrateful, loud, and egotistical. We make potty jokes. We complain. And yet, they don't lose faith in us. They love us despite our indifference. They stand by us, defend us, worry about and nourish us—day in and day out.

I don't think the question of how they do it—be it Mary's faith or the conviction of my mom and wife—needs to be answered. God gave us these great women in our lives, as He blesses us in so many ways. It's just our job to say thank you and to hope we can earn their faith in return.

Verse: "My soul glorifies the Lord and my spirit rejoices in God my Savior, for he has been mindful of the humble state of his servant. From now on all generations will call me blessed, for the Mighty One has done great things for me—holy is his name. His mercy extends to those who fear him, from generation to generation" (Luke 1:46–50).

Further Reading:

> Proverbs 31
> Luke 1:35
> John 19:26–27

Prayer: Dear Lord, thank You for Mary's example. She is the embodiment of the trust I seek in my relationship with You. She is the inspiration to honor the women in my life and to seek compassion in everything I do. Amen.

CHAPTER FIVE

Lifelong Learners

Jesus was primarily a teacher. But it's difficult to imagine Him sending home a classroom letter to His disciples' parents like the one that came home from my child's school.

> Dear Parents/Guardians,
> We've had a successful start to the school year. There's nothing more inspiring to see than a classroom of third-grade children eager to learn. Their little faces light up when they grasp a new concept—their hands fly into the air when it's time to share what they know. A rewarding experience for me, to say the least.
>
> We have had a few problems, however, with our lunch lines recently. Namely, children have been taking cuts. While I do not condone this behavior, would you please remind your child that it's not nice to say: "No cuts, no buts, no coconuts." The first graders caught on to this and wouldn't stop saying it, even when the mayor stopped by for Make a Difference Day.

The class enjoyed our field trip to the veterinarian last week as part of our Fins, Fur, and Feathers unit. Thanks to those parents who helped chaperone. As you have undoubtedly heard by now, we had the unique opportunity (not to mention surprise) to see a cat neutered. Of course, I sincerely hope those children who threw up are feeling much better. Our next field trip will be to the city sewer as part of our Workers in My Neighborhood unit.

Academics are progressing smoothly in class. I would ask, however, that you don't do your children's homework for them. There's nothing worse than doing your children's homework ... except perhaps doing your children's homework incorrectly. My "frown face" stamp has received quite a workout.

Please also be aware that all next week the school nurse will be vaccinating those children whose shot records are not up to date. The nurse requests that you prepare your child mentally for this traumatic event. She recently had knee surgery, and she won't be able to chase after and tackle frightened children.

As for the Lost and Found, the custodian wants to remind parents to check through the items in the basket and take home what items might belong to your family. The basket has also been recently moved from the library to the covered shed outside so that those students reading books don't have to plug their noses anymore.

Finally, the PTA has asked me to pass on their gratitude this month. They would like to thank all the parents who recently contributed their time and money to the PTA school fundraiser. The cookie dough sale was quite a success. The money raised will help us paint over the naughty words in the boys' bathroom, plus replace the science equipment that caught on fire during Mr. Jorgenson's Bunsen burner demonstration. If you are in the building and get a chance, please stop by Mr. Jorgenson's classroom and give him a few encouraging words. The doctor said it would be three weeks before his eyebrows grow back. He could use the moral support.

Well, that's all from the third-grade class. If I don't see you personally before then, I hope each and every one of you has a joyous and happy month.

Sincerely yours,

Ms. Goodesteem

P.S. Report cards will be issued Friday. Some of you should rest before then.

Jesus also didn't have to contend with school photos for His disciples. Meanwhile, our kids' school photos came home. And—good news—they were better than the previous year's ... even though one child had his eyes shut in the picture and another looked like she might faint. Boy, what a relief!

In years past, they were much worse. In fact, let's just say that they weren't allowed into the yearbook because school officials worried they might scare the kindergartners.

Don't get me wrong: my children were cute and adorable. But they couldn't seem to take a decent school photo to save their lives. For example, they had the loveliest smiles … until they got in front of a camera lens. Then, they looked like a cross between someone smiling and someone who accidentally farted in class.

If I didn't know better, I'd think that the photographers were telling my kids, "Okay, on the count of three say 'Cheese'"—then clicking the shot on two.

It was this way since preschool. I remember when I showed my mom my son's first school photo. She took one look at the odd expression on his face and asked if he was getting enough fiber.

It was hard on the rest of my family as well. After all, it's tradition to put photos of your nieces and nephews or grandchildren on the mantel. I know, because we have pictures of our six nephews and niece prominently displayed on the top of our piano. My extended family, however, tends to like cheerful pictures instead of mug shots. So each year when I passed out the photos of my kids, they'd say things like "Eeeeew" or "Thanks, I was looking for a picture to put in the shed."

I got used to it. I could always count on the photos being a disaster. That was why my family had a standing retake order with the school.

Unfortunately, even the retakes needed retakes.

Curiously, my children didn't have problems in all photographic environments. They did just fine in pictures taken at the beach, at a school concert, or opening gifts on Christmas morning. They looked natural and normal anywhere they weren't expected to smile on demand.

The only part I don't understand, even now, is why something can't be done about this. Who takes these photos at the schools? Where do the principals find these photographers? Don't they have little tricks of the trade to get kids like mine to look their best? Or, in fact, do they have ulterior motives? Maybe they *like* taking these screwy photos. Maybe the school photographers get together at a convention to share these disasters.

"And in this next photo of Claire Swarner, I went for a style that seems to say, 'Look, Ma, I'm swallowing my tongue.'"

Oh well, it's not like school photos had much bearing on the future careers of my children. After all, I knew they could always be hand models.

I wonder, though, how many days Jesus had like my son's kindergarten teacher experienced in her class one fateful spring day. For weeks, the students had had the unique opportunity to incubate chicken eggs in their classroom. The teacher led the children through the entire birth process so they could prepare to witness firsthand this miracle of life.

Eventually, the kindies could hear the chicks chirping inside their eggs, and in one case, a chick had started to peck its way to freedom. Everyone was excited, and they couldn't wait for the babies to arrive in the next day or two.

Then tragedy struck. Between the morning and afternoon kindergarten classes, in the process of the teacher and custodian trying to better distribute the eggs inside the incubator, the heat was accidentally raised in the pen. As any good employee of KFC will tell you, that's a recipe for well done.

The next day, instead of watching the fluffy yellow chicks run around inside the incubator, my son and his stunned classmates attended a burial near the school's playground.

It was still on his mind three years later at a family dinner. "Grandpa, guess what? Our baby chickens died."

I have to figure that probably 95 percent of my son's kindergarten class (when polled as adults and asked about their early childhood memories) will list the baby-chick genocide as their major kindergarten memory. You just typically don't forget something dramatic like that.

Regardless of what my son's kindergarten teacher taught that year, the great programs she arranged, the field trips, the classroom activities—her legacy of this kindergarten class will be the tragic Chick Deaths of Kindergarten.

My son at the sports bar with his friends: "When I was in kindergarten and our baby chicks were starting to peck open their shells with their cute little beaks, my teacher accidentally cranked up the heat and sent them all to their poultry graves. It was really sad, and then my best friend Joey Littlejohn yelled really loud, 'Yum, fried chicken.'"

Jesus is an amazing teacher. I wish I'd had just 1 percent of His talent when it came to teaching my kids math. No one in my family ever went looking for me when they had an equation to solve. They'd ask their friends, neighbors, and grandfathers before they'd seek my advice. Heck, I think my son once asked the cat to explain X.

I'm that bad with numbers.

When my children needed help on their math homework and I was the only adult in the room, they'd say things like "Where's Mom?" and "I suppose I'll just take a zero on this assignment."

I've never been good with math concepts. Admittingly, that may have something to do with the fact that I didn't pay attention in math class as a kid. That, and my parents still refuse to admit they dropped me on my head when I was young.

I won't go so far as to say that I chose journalism because I am math impaired—mainly because statistics (math) was a requirement for my journalism degree … and yeah, I nearly failed it.

The funny part is that my parents could have sucked at math and I would have never known it, because the relationship back then between parents and schoolwork was nearly nonexistent. Not so anymore. These days, parents are on the front lines when it comes to school homework. You are expected to sign assignment planners, keep track of time reading with your kids, and be that go-to source for homework help. Math is no exception.

Don't get me wrong, I was fine up to the point when my children passed the fifth grade. I can do division and multiplication, and I could even "manipulate" those colored blocks (whatever that was about). But starting in sixth grade, the kids entered the beginning of algebra, and I was soon lost. I made up every excuse I could think of to save face:

1. "Ow! I think a bug flew in my eye!"
2. "This isn't the math we did when *I* was a kid."
3. "Who wants ice cream?"

After a while, my children figured it out.

It's hard to admit, but I ceased to be the superman in my children's lives. Where I could once handle every question and situation that came my way, I became lucky to get it right half of the time. As I've gotten older, I've noticed more and more that they do certain things better than I can. And that's tough to get used to.

I think it was a little disappointing for them as well. That transition from child to young adult is full of many mysteries, including, "How did my dad, who once knew everything, suddenly get so stupid?"

I guess that's just how biology works in order to move kids into adulthood … and maybe part of the trouble they have in holding on to their faith is that, as they get older, they see things as less cut and dried. I am confident enough to be okay with the fact that I'm not as good at math as they are. I did, however, get a little tired of having to constantly fish out my college diploma to prove to them that I actually graduated.

Not to say that all education takes place in the schools. Have you noticed that potty training a child is now a spectator sport?

When moms and dads start the momentous task of transitioning their kids from diapers to alfresco, parents like to make a really big deal about it. They clap loudly, call the relatives, make posters. It's a huge event, carried out with the enthusiasm of pro football cheerleaders. I half expect one of these days to see dads holding up ballpark foam fingers that read: "My Son Went #1!"

My kids have been out of diapers for many years, but I never bought into publicizing the educational process. I've always subscribed to the school of thought that says toilet discussions belong in the home, or between a plumber and me.

Not so in the case of my sister.

One time, my mom was in the car with my wife and me, and her cell phone rang.

"Hello?" she answered. "Yes … *Really?* … Okay, put him on the phone. (Pause.) Hi, sweetie. Mommy says you went potty on the *big-boy chair* … You did? … That's neat … Yes, I'm so proud of you—what? (Pause.) Wow! You even hit the Cheerio?"

I glanced over at my wife, perplexed. "Cheerio?"

She nodded. "Parents put them in the toilet so their kids can try to hit them with their … their …"

"Oh," I said. "With their … their …"

"Exactly."

I'm glad neither of us had to say it.

"Thanks for calling me," my mom said, finishing her call. "Here, tell your Uncle Ken what you did."

"Mom!"

I suppose you can't really blame most moms and dads, or grandmas, for being excited. After two to four years of changing diapers, a little encouragement is *well* in order.

But some parents go off the deep end, I think. Like at the grocery store.

"Jimmy, tell the nice man what you did this morning."

I looked at the woman with her son standing ahead of me in the "10 items or less" line and raised my eyebrows.

"I went potty on the potty chair, mister."

"Really?" I said, wondering what to do next. Should I give him a high five? Share the news with the guy standing behind me? "Hey, this kid up here went potty—pass it on." I wasn't sure, so I gave him a nickel.

Of course, I'm glad this kind of stuff doesn't happen in the adult world.

> Frank: Ken, I went potty in the executive bathroom for the very first time!
> Me: Wow, Frank. I'd like to recognize you during the staff meeting. Can I tell them you hit the Cheerio?

I shouldn't complain, I suppose. Even if it's not the way I did it, there's nothing wrong with encouraging young people to set goals and accomplish them.

I tried to be supportive of my sister by doing my part to get excited about my nephew going to the bathroom. As the family was gathered at my mom's house, my sister and her son came bursting in the room, smiling from dimple to dimple.

"Well, tell them," my sister prodded.

"I just went potty in the potty chair," my nephew announced.

I led The Wave.

REFLECTION

How would Jesus have handled the extra-crispy chicks in the incubator? Probably in the same way He always ministered and taught—with grace and mercy. I would like to have seen Him there with the kindergartners, comforting them, offering His compassion. One of my favorite quotes from the Bible is this: "Let the little children come to me, and do not hinder them, for the kingdom of God belongs to such as these" (Mark 10:14).

Our childhood educations were memorable, weren't they? We have these images and events from decades ago that still stick with us today. Can you imagine, at a time when formal school didn't exist for the vast majority of children, how unforgettable the ministry of Jesus must have been for His followers? How revolutionary His teachings must have been? Well, I guess we do know its impact, don't we? We have the Gospels.

There's an innocence that I believe many of us miss from our childhoods. Perhaps this is why our memories of school are still so powerful. It's why we sometimes ache for those days long gone—we want that "easier" faith back. I loved that time when I devotedly and unequivocally believed in things that I couldn't see, especially

God. It was so freeing and comforting. I need to go back to school with the Bible as my textbook and strengthen the faith I once so effortlessly enjoyed.

> **I need to go back to school with the Bible as my textbook and strengthen the faith I once so effortlessly enjoyed.**

Why is it so difficult to remember to spend ten minutes a night reading the Bible, and yet so easy to remember to watch a favorite show? Is it because the lessons learned in the Bible are tough to swallow? If we read it, will we feel compelled to change? I put a Bible on my nightstand after I wrote this chapter. That was a big first step. Now I need to listen for the first-period bell and start studying!

Verse: "The fear of the LORD is the beginning of knowledge, but fools despise wisdom and instruction" (Prov. 1:7).

Further Reading:

> Ecclesiastes 7
> Matthew 7
> Romans 12

Prayer: Today, I will look honestly at my actions, taking to heart Jesus' teachings so that I can find peace and honor through change. Guide me, Lord. I will listen to that little voice in my head and truly examine myself. By Your grace, I will be the better person I know I can be. Amen.

CHAPTER SIX

Rock-a-Bye Jesus

Because of the whole miraculous-conception thing, Mary never had to tell anyone she and Joseph were "trying" to have a baby.

So I was confused when a friend of mine told me recently that he and his wife were trying to have a baby. Wanting to be helpful, I replied, "That's nice. Don't you know how?"

I always chuckle when two perfectly healthy people use the "try" word. It's almost as if they plan to do it on a trapeze.

> Wife: Don't worry, sweetie, there's a net below us.
> Husband: *Ahhhhhhhhhh!*

As my dad is fond of saying: "We never tried to have a baby in my day … other than, maybe, to try *not* to have a baby."

It's true. People can try to bench-press four hundred pounds. They can try to lose weight. They can even try to double the value of their stock portfolio. But when it comes to having a baby, it's pretty straightforward.

Now, before those with fertility issues bite my head off, I am, of course, talking about people who use the "try" word before they have any indication they can't conceive a baby. Those who struggle to conceive can use any word they like. In fact, they should have exclusive rights over that word. But that's not my point.

The problem I have with people announcing that they are "trying" to have a baby is that I feel some things are better left unsaid. After all, what are the rest of us supposed to say when these proclamations are made? Isn't it just another way of telling people, "By the way, after we play cards tonight with you folks, Frank and I are going home and having sex"?

It's not like we can be honest when they tell us.

> Person 1: Bob and I are trying to have a baby.
> Person 2: Eeeew.

No, we have to get excited for the person.

> Person 1: And I'm ovulating off the charts.
> Person 2: Great. Maybe you'd be more comfortable sitting on a wooden chair.

I'm probably from the old school, but I don't think it's good etiquette to be walking around telling everyone you see that your evening hours are being spent making babies. And believe me, I have known people who haven't felt constrained in any form or fashion from telling people they were "trying." They make their announcements at PTA, school choir concerts, hot yoga sessions—even at church. It's as if they are the first people to actually "try" this.

> Person 1: This may come as a total shock to you, but Bill and I have decided to boldly go where no one has gone before. Tonight, after we binge-watch *Ozark*, we will retire to our bedroom, light some candles, pray, and then conceive the very first child as God intended. We are going to … brace yourselves … you know … try to have a baby.
>
> Person 2: Will that be paper or plastic?

I never told people my wife and I were planning to make children. I just assumed people would get that fact when we announced my wife was pregnant. Sure, some people might have thought we hadn't planned the pregnancy, but I was fine leaving such things open for interpretation.

After all, if we were meant to make formal announcements, wouldn't Hallmark have a card for that? Something like "Roses are red, violets are blue, we're trying to have a baby, how about you?"

If you are a parent, then you most likely started when your child was at the baby stage—or as I like to call it, the first real test of a marriage … and of sanity.

There is little we know of Mary and Joseph's marriage. Nor do we know much about Jesus as a baby. Of course, seeing that Jesus was perfect, we have to assume He slept through the night, ate on schedule, never cried in His crib, and folded His own clothes and put them away.

Mary and Joseph, therefore, had little reason to negotiate chores with each other.

It could be said that the most complicated aspect for two regular parents trying to manage as equals is keeping track of whose turn it is regarding the tasks of child raising.

During the baby years, my wife and I could rattle off exactly how many diapers we had changed versus how many diapers the other had changed ... going back at least 346 hours at any one time. We also knew where we stood on the number of baths we'd given, how many times we'd put the kids in their pajamas, and whose turn it was to rinse out the Diaper Genie.

Statistics like these aren't, however, kept for scientific reasons, or to be charted in a child's baby book. Instead, they come in handy when it's time to argue whose turn it is to complete the next chore.

I remember our first baby like it was yesterday.

> My wife: Sweetie, it's your turn to change the baby's diaper.
>
> Me: It's *not* my turn. This morning, I got up at the crack of dawn and rocked the baby for an hour, changed two poopie diapers, bathed the kid, washed out the diaper bag, and threw my back out chiseling dry Cheerios off the linoleum floor.
>
> My wife: That might be true, but yesterday, I changed *three* poopie diapers, fed and burped the baby, cleaned out the car seat, washed twenty-eight spit-up rags, made an appointment with the pediatrician, played two hours of peekaboo, and

> strained carrots. And if that wasn't enough, I had
> a nightmare last night that I was eaten alive by a
> rabid Huggies box. It's your turn!

My wife had me on that extra poopie diaper.

Having friends and family who also parented equally and nego-tiated in numbers was somewhat comforting, if only to know that we were not alone.

I was over at my sister's house for my nephew's birthday, and just before the candles were lit, a familiar smell wafted through the room. My sister's youngest had left a gift, and not the kind anyone wanted to unwrap.

Both my sister and her husband looked exhaustedly at each other.

"I changed the last one," my brother-in-law stated.

"In your dreams," my sister retorted.

The conversation went back and forth like that for a couple of minutes. My neck started to hurt from trying to follow it. The room also got riper. I think my mom finally changed my nephew's diaper. That might have been their tactic all along.

In fact, there are a number of strategies to get out of pulling diaper duty (pun intended).

There are the tried-and-true games called …

Retracing Our Steps

In this type of match, both parents employ whatever means of persuasion they can find to attempt to prove they changed the last diaper. Options include flowcharts, witnesses, and the detective game, also known as "Whose hands smell the most like fresh baby wipes?"

Evidence is always key to the conversation.

> Husband: No, honey, I clearly remember changing the last diaper. See, my eyes are still watering.

It All Stacks Up

Other times, it isn't a matter of who went last but who is left behind. In this scenario, one spouse has spent the day away enjoying real adult conversations, uninterrupted meals, and time to daydream, while the other parent was stuck home with two kids in Pampers.

> Husband: I'm home, dear.
> Wife: Hi, honey. Did you have a nice golf game? By the way, you owe me seventeen diaper changes.
> Husband: Are you feeding the kids chili?

The "I Didn't Notice" Game

On some occasions, it's not about keeping track of who changed the last diaper but of reverting back to the old refrain: "Ye who smelt it must change it."

> Wife: Honey, didn't you notice that the baby needed changing? I could smell it clear back in the bedroom.
> Husband: I couldn't smell anything.

Wife: Then why are you breathing into the couch cushion?

I Pulled a Hammy

Husband: (plugging his nose) Oh, mercy—this diaper is going to be a doozy. Look, the neighbors are all out on their front lawns trying to figure out what the smell is. I sure am glad I changed the last two today. You're up, sweetheart.

Wife: (knocking her own head into the wall) Can't. I need to go to the emergency room—I think I have a concussion. Don't worry, I'll drive myself.

The Escape Route

Finally, when all else fails, spouses can join forces and tackle the issue together.

Husband: Okay, we'll be back around 9:00 p.m.

Wife: There's food in the fridge, and our number is on the counter.

Babysitter: Okay, but what's that smell?

Husband: (under his breath) Honey, run!

Mostly, my wife and I played the numbers game. The problem, of course, with trading off is that it's rife with corruption. Nothing stops a wife, for example, from lying to her husband as he returns from the grocery store, saying that she changed three diapers in his absence … even if he had been gone only fifteen minutes.

> Wife: I think I got carpal tunnel syndrome on that
> last one ... You, *gasp*, have the next three.

The other problem is that, at times, this could change two seemingly normal and well-adjusted adults into imbeciles squabbling like children, which is very unchristianlike.

Still, it was the best system we found for getting those diapers changed.

Of course, I'd like to say that things relaxed when we had teenagers, who (supposedly) could do more things for themselves. But as my wife and I discovered, they didn't. I remember the day I told my wife it was her turn to "listen to the general angst of our middle son."

> My wife: Sorry. I already listened to thirty minutes
> of "Mom, you're ruining my life" this morning.
> You're up!
> Me: Dang!

I decided to remember that one.

Speaking of Mary and Joseph: as any kid who attends Sunday school can tell you, Mary rode on the back of a donkey to get to the stable to deliver Jesus. My sister didn't have it so easy.

As a number of us from the family gathered in my sister's hospital room to see her new baby, she recounted her trip to the emergency room earlier that day. She woke up around 4:00 a.m. feeling the early pangs of labor. For the next two hours, she and her husband, Bill, timed the contractions, and at around 7:00 a.m., they decided it was time to leave for the hospital.

On the way, however, Bill announced that he needed to stop at Starbucks for coffee.

"Excuse me?" my sister said. "I'm in labor, remember?"

"But I might get a headache if I don't have my morning coffee," Bill explained.

My sister did a double take. "And while you're inside Starbucks, I might have to ask a stranger to cut my umbilical cord. What's your point?"

Bill promised her that he'd order the coffee to go.

Anyway, next thing Debbie knew, her husband was hustling into their local coffee shop.

Inside, the baristas recognized Bill, knew he was expecting a second son, and asked when the baby was due.

"Today," Bill said, ordering his Americano.

"Today?" the cashier asked.

Bill nodded. "Yep, Debbie is already in labor."

Everyone offered up congratulations.

"So, where's your wife?" someone finally asked.

"Out there," Bill said pointing toward the parking lot, where my sister was sitting in the car, puffing heavily through a contraction … in her pajamas.

"Was she okay with stopping here?" the barista asked, amazement in her voice.

"Not really," Bill answered sheepishly.

"Yeah, that's probably why she isn't waving back."

As my sister continued telling the story, Bill looked around at the disapproving faces in the hospital room. "What's wrong with that?" he asked. "I had to have my coffee."

I think his mother best summed it up when she announced, "I'm ashamed of my son."

In his defense, Bill told us that he had been through the labor drill before with his first son, and therefore, he knew he had time for a quick cup. He also pointed out that he *did* ask my sister if she wanted something to drink too.

Frankly, Bill could have chalked up the pit stop to his preparedness plan, stating that in order to be at his best as my sister's husband and coach, the coffee was a much-needed stimulant, for the solitary benefit of my sister. That would have sounded reasonable ... if he hadn't also ordered a biscotto.

Finally, Bill looked to me, the only other male in the room over eleven, and asked if I agreed with him.

"I'm not saying a word," I replied, looking around at the women. "We're outnumbered."

I also explained that if I was ever having a heart attack, I wasn't calling him for a ride to the hospital.

When one of my sons was in high school, he brought home a baby from school. It was one of those lifelike computerized dolls that cries intermittently when it needs a diaper change, something to eat, or to drive Grandpa Ken insane.

My son was handed the doll in his health class. For two days, he carried it with him everywhere. Inside the robo-baby, sophisticated sensors recorded everything from my son's response time in attending to the baby's needs to how carefully he supported the newborn's neck.

At first, I was all for the project. After all, like any parent, I wanted to scare the beejeebers out of my children any way I could to prevent them from having sex before they were employed, married, and responsible. The doll is designed to do just that. It demonstrates—through a powerful, shrilling cry—the work (and noise) involved in raising a newborn. It shows a teenager the very real consequences of pregnancy.

Believe me, after the project was over, that message had rung *loud* and clear at my house ... for *me*, that is.

Even then, I was far enough from the baby game that I had forgotten how disturbing those midnight feedings could be. If the robo-baby wasn't waking me up with its cries—a cry by the way that sounded like twenty seals being beaten to a pulp—then I was lying in bed nervously waiting for the baby to start screaming.

I lost my patience around 4:00 a.m. the second night.

"Dad, I can't get it to stop crying!" my son exclaimed after rushing into my room for the seventh time that evening.

I mumbled something to the effect of "*Grmhr* ... it's your baby ... *armph*."

"But I don't know what to do," he said. "It won't stop crying!"

I rubbed the sleep out of my eyes. "Bummer! You should have thought of that before you had sex!"

"I haven't *had* sex, Dad!"

"Oh," I replied groggily. "Maybe I should have thought of this before *I* had sex."

Luckily, my wife brought the baby into our bed, and she managed to calm us all down. Which worked until Chucky got hungry again and his cries startled the milkman dropping off the Thursday order.

It's amazing how quickly I had fallen out of the baby routine. Where I was once climbing groggily out of bed to manage the midnight feedings, now I was pleading for my middle schooler to put his baby in the trunk of my car.

> **It's amazing how quickly I had fallen out of the baby routine. Where I was once climbing groggily out of bed to manage the midnight feedings, now I was pleading for my middle schooler to put his baby in the trunk of my car.**

Needless to say, we survived (barely). The next day, I even wrote a supportive note to my son's health-class teacher.

"Dear Mr. Thompson. Here's your baby back. You win. When you pass around the abstinence-pledge forms, sign my son up … and me too."

I figured that should do it.

REFLECTION

An amazing thing happens when you have a baby: your instincts change. At least, I know mine did. In the first minute of holding each of my children, I realized that I would give my life for them without reservation. My love for them is enduring and complete. Since they were babies, I could not imagine my life without them. If need be, I would die so that they could live.

Christian martyrs had that kind of love for Jesus Christ. Throughout the ages, they gave their lives for the Father, Son, and Holy Spirit, also without reservation. In the early days of Christianity, they followed Jesus knowing it surely meant their deaths. They marched into the Colosseum to face lions and tigers rather than denounce their faith in the Lord. Their love was enduring and complete. And those stories have continued to the present day. Even in the twenty-first century, there are Christians putting their lives on the line to worship and glorify God.

I'm not sure I would die for my faith. I am sad to write that and ashamed that that is true. I'm afraid I wouldn't sacrifice myself and my responsibilities to my family in order to uphold my Christian beliefs. Maybe if I were in the situation, my choice would surprise me. But right now, it seems that if being a Christian meant death, I'd likely hide who I was.

How about you?

I *want* to love Jesus enough to lay my life down in His name. I am on that road, and one day, I hope I can say I am ready. Attaining that level of commitment to God and enriching my life beyond anything I can possibly comprehend is the ultimate way to live, paying dividends in this life and beyond. In theory, I want to give my life to honor His.

When my kids were toddlers, we played the game "How much do Mommy and Daddy love you?" We'd stretch our arms out as far as they would go and announce, "This much!" I need to play that game with Jesus!

Verse: "Then Jesus said to his disciples, 'Whoever wants to be my disciple must deny themselves and take up their cross and follow me'" (Matt. 16:24).

Further Reading:

> Matthew 10
> Acts 12
> 1 Peter 2

Prayer: Lord, grant me the fortitude to give my life for You. Even though I am not ready to walk into the Colosseum, I am prepared to live my life for Your glory. Help me today to bear witness to Your teachings, no matter the personal cost. Show me the path to love all mankind even when that requires sacrifice. I stand boldly today, my arms stretched wide, to be Your disciple in all ways. Amen.

CHAPTER SEVEN

The Patience of Job

"The Almighty is beyond our reach and exalted in power; in his justice and great righteousness, he does not oppress" (Job 37:23).

That's from the final chapters of the book of Job.

In our cultural lexicon is the phrase *the patience of Job*. You've undoubtedly heard that Job had a rock-solid faith in God. To prove to Satan that a pious man like Job would not lose faith in God even if he was brought to his knees by the Almighty, the Lord did just that. He took everything from Job, including his health.

When our kids were young, I reread the story of Job in the Bible, and it gave me a lot to think about as a parent. After all, Job had infinite patience, and I, well, don't.

When God made me, I think He pulled my wires too tight. There has to be a sound reason why I short-circuited so fast when the kids couldn't find their shoes (again), relayed important messages in baby voices, or sang seventeen nail-biting choruses of the diarrhea song.

Have you seen those parents waiting patiently in a crowded toy store as their children touch every single product as if they'll win a prize for leaving their fingerprints on everything? I can't stand that. If I was in a store with my children for more than five minutes, I began to sweat. Ten minutes, and I was crying into an Elmo bath set.

Oh, sure, patient parents make it look easy.

One time, I witnessed a dad sit in a restaurant while his kids shot spit wads with a straw at his face, and not once did I see him flinch.

I wouldn't even consider letting my kids have a straw. If I had, they would probably have pulled their wagons into the street and thrown a parade in my honor.

What I had the least patience for, I suppose, was listening to the children's knock-knock jokes. They went something like this: "Knock-knock. Who's there? Salad. Salad who? Don't you want some salad?"

Can you imagine listening to 107 of those, back to back during a family car trip? I suppose I shouldn't complain—I heard only 88 of them as we cruised along Interstate 5. That's when I clenched my jaws so tight I grinded the enamel off my two front teeth and passed out from the pain.

I never thought much about patience before I became a father. I suppose it is one of those things I never realized I had until I'd lost it. Since misplacing my composure, however, I started trying to figure out why there were other parents who still had theirs. Were they sipping at the vanilla extract when no one was looking?

Take for example my neighbor. I really envied the guy. He was the Fred Rogers of the street. I never once saw the man lose his patience … and he had six kids.

One day, however, my son came home early from playing at this neighbor's house.

"I thought you were with the Rogers kid?" I asked him.

"Their last name is Gregory, Dad! Anyway, Mr. Gregory overheard us telling knock-knock jokes, and he ran out of the house in his pajamas. They're waiting for the police to find him."

When he came back on his own, I called George Gregory, and we chartered a support group.

Maybe it's just a matter of time before everyone eventually cracks.

Still, I began trying harder to follow Job's example. At Denny's, I even let my kids each have a straw. I'm still sweeping the ticker tape off the street. Boy, that really tried my patience!

Of course, part of the patience problem came from the constant racket. I bet if researchers did a study on parents, they'd discover that, collectively, most of us haven't had one single, important, creative, and/or probing thought in years.

We're all practically clueless.

It's no wonder. Who can think with all the noise children make? The constant questions—the running and screaming—the music blaring from every room in the house (occupied or not). This immutable clamor makes contemplative thought impossible. Parents can't even manage reading directions, composing a shopping list, or stringing two words together. (Incidentally, it always seemed to be during a crisis in my home, like when the dishwasher flooded or a tree fell on the house, that my kids really shot for the stars and started a sixteen-piece saucepan orchestra in the kitchen.)

Parents are complete morons, really. No longer able to think, we just stare off into space, only able to get through the day by pure animal instinct. This is why you'll see a parent at the grocery store staring blankly at the frozen orange juice while her screaming children climb in and out of the grocery cart. The mom doesn't twitch a muscle. She can't. She just desperately clutches her shopping list and stares at the freezer window, trying unsuccessfully to grapple with the thought: *Do ... we ... need ... juice?*

People without children often misread these situations. They'll push their cart past the mom and think the poor woman is dreaming of being alone on a tropical island. The rest of us, of course, know exactly what's going on. She's caught in a complete, helpless, catatonic state ... sort of like the juice.

It's sad what happens to parents. Door-to-door salesmen witness this every day.

> Salesman: Good afternoon, sir. Do you have a home alarm system?
> Me: Uhhhh.
> Salesman: Should I take that as a no, sir? Or does the drool mean yes?

I learned to steal some moments alone, just to think. For example, I'd take a slow walk to the mailbox, hide in the shower, turn on the vacuum cleaner, or run down the street pretending to chase the cat. When I really wanted to get crazy, instead of turning to drugs and alcohol, I'd find a quiet place to feel the rush of forming a complete thought. I'm sure people saw me at the library ... giggling to myself.

I suppose there is money to be made in all this. I could rent my house out to those professionals who might benefit from the noise. I could start a trade school for people who need to learn how to filter out distractions, such as bomb defusers, safecrackers, and school bus drivers.

Little good that would've done me in my job, though. I'm a writer, so I need a quiet atmosphere to concentrate. When I don't get it, I make mistakes. When I don't get it, I make mistakes.

It's not that I didn't try to be more patient. Job had four friends to give him advice (okay, not the right kind—but they cared). Me? I had to turn to resolutions and other promises.

I don't know why I put such stock in making New Year's resolutions, but I feel guilty if I don't at least try to improve. And like many red-blooded parents, the part of my life that I felt the most challenged in was patience with my children.

One year, I told my wife I wanted a New Year's resolution aimed at being a better dad.

"What do you want to do better?" she asked.

"I was thinking about how I interact with the children."

"What does that mean?"

"Well," I said, "I raise my voice too many times."

"Does something else work?"

"You aren't helping."

She placed a gentle hand on my shoulder. "Listen, why don't you ask the kids what they think before picking a resolution that doesn't matter to them?"

I liked that suggestion. A little while later, I returned.

"What was their idea?" my wife asked.

"They want a later bedtime."

"That's a resolution?"

"Not a good one," I answered. "Our kids had no idea what a resolution was. So I was really patient, and I took the time to explain the whole process and how it needs to be about me."

"What did they say?"

"They don't care when I go to bed."

I decided to go with not raising my voice. I even wrote it down on a note card and pinned it on the wall next to my bed. Then, beginning January 1, I changed my ways.

All in all, I thought the first two hours went relatively well. Mostly because I watched football.

Before long, however, I was confronted with misbehaving children. Somehow, without raising my voice, I had to get my children's attention.

I tried stamping my feet, snapping my fingers, clearing my throat—nothing helped. Finally, I grabbed a Happy Meal whistle and blew it really hard. It didn't get the kids' attention, but the dog has had better behavior since then.

By early afternoon, I was doing all I could to keep the words inside me. When I'd want to shout, I covered my mouth, bit my tongue, or munched a handful of crackers. I even slapped myself. It hurt.

I also kept catching myself before I raised my voice. I'd go "Ack" or "Wha" or "Uh."

My son noticed this and said something.

"Dad, are you okay?"

"Yes. Why?"

"It's just that you were making funny noises."

"So?"

"So, that's how the cat sounds just before she pukes a hair ball."

By late afternoon, I was sweating under the strain. I even tried really hard to keep my voice down when I caught my son bouncing on the furniture.

Then, suddenly, the house came to a standstill. Everyone was staring at me.

"What?" I asked.

"You just shouted," my wife replied.

"No, I didn't," I argued. "I was talking to myself."

"Do you often yell at yourself to stop horsing around?"

"Yes. I'm a very bad boy."

Finally, nineteen hours into the New Year, my children punched a hole into the playroom wall, and I lost it completely.

"Dad, I thought you weren't going to raise your voice anymore?" my son said.

"That was before I knew you'd do something like this!"

"So, should we discuss bedtimes?" he asked.

"Okay."

I needed prayer for times like these too:

At 10:00 a.m.: My wife and I, two seemingly normal parents with all the best intentions to have fun and accomplish a few errands, arrive at a suburban shopping mall with our children.

10:02 a.m.: I tell the children to stop touching the merchandise.

10:12 a.m.: Tuckered out from ten minutes of shopping, my child demands to be carried. When I explain the enormous health benefits of using his feet, he slumps to the ground like a wet noodle and almost trips an elderly couple walking behind us.

10:13 a.m.: I carry my child through the next two stores.

10:25 a.m.: After the seventh time my son grabs a store rack while still in my arms, nearly dislocating my shoulder, I put him back on the ground.

10:29 a.m.: I tell the children to stop touching the merchandise.

10:31 a.m.: My other son announces it's his turn to be carried. I tell him he will need to wait until I consult with my chiropractor, so in protest, he wet-noodles on the escalator.

10:32 a.m.: I carry my son through the next four stores.

10:50 a.m.: I tell my children to stop touching the merchandise.

10:55 a.m.: We stop at the food court for something to drink, which is relaxing—until the children start to fight and knock *my* drink into *my* lap. As the kids happily sip their beverages, I look like I wet myself.

11:15 a.m.: I forget I'm walking around the mall looking like I wet myself, until my child shouts loudly, "Hey, Dad, did you go pee-pee in your pants?"

11:17 a.m.: I buy gum so I can have a bag to carry in front of my wet pants.

11:25 a.m.: I tell my children to stop touching the merchandise.

11:45 a.m.: As my wife tries on a couple of outfits in a dressing room, I grab the only chair in sight as the children hide inside the clothes racks. As shoppers reach for the hangers, my kids make startling duck calls. I walk over to stop them, and my youngest steals my seat.

11:50 a.m.: I join my wife in the dressing room.

"Are you having fun?" I ask.

"Yes," she replies, trying on a new dress. "Are you?"

"Of course," I answer. "Maybe some nagging back spasms and the misconception of a bladder-control problem, but nothing a blow to the head wouldn't cure."

She stares at me with concern in her eyes. "Honey, now answer me honestly, do I look fat in this outfit?"

12:05 p.m.: I tell my children to stop touching the merchandise.

12:30 p.m.: As I'm enjoying a couple of solitary moments testing aftershave fragrances, my son screams at the top of his lungs. All heads turn in his direction, which wouldn't be so bad if he didn't also have a goofy grin on his face and a size-44 bra held to his tummy. Actually, I take that back. The low point was when he shouted, "Hey, Dad! I look like Great-Grandma!"

12:41 p.m.: I tell my children to stop touching the merchandise ... from where I'm lying on the floor.

And what about those school-supplies lists to try a person's patience?

Every year, my children came home from school with their supply lists. Every year, I was left thinking, *Don't the astronauts go into orbit with less stuff?*

Back then, the lists were enormous, and I know they've only grown since. Pens, mechanical pencils, highlighters, earthquake kits, calculators, student planners, protractors, spiral notebooks. When I was a kid, I could carry all my supplies from the store in my arms. Today, children need pack mules.

Of course, my wife didn't bat an eye when the lists came home. She just gathered up our kids and headed off to the store. And I did my fatherly duty and followed them.

(I had to follow them because when they heard I wanted to go, they left without me.)

When I finally caught up, I asked my wife why she didn't wait.

She took me aside. "Ken, the kids and I thought it might be easier on you if you didn't have to watch the money being spent."

"You're happy about these huge lists?"

"No," she answered, "but your complaining about the money doesn't help."

"I don't—"

My wife raised an eyebrow. "Last year, at the checkout register, you told the kids we'd have to cut costs at home to pay for the supplies."

"So?"

"So, you said you hoped they didn't mind eating dirt for dinner."

I blanched. "If I promise to tag along quietly, can I stay?"

She reluctantly agreed. And for the first twenty minutes, I was a perfect angel. We bought some loose-leaf paper, a couple of glue sticks, some number two pencils. I even made each child go back and get an extra eraser. What can I say? I splurged.

Then my wife scanned the school list and said, "We need two boxes of 102 crayons."

"*What?*" I exclaimed. "Didn't we just get markers, paints, pens, and colored pencils? Now crayons? Who's running this school—Picasso?"

My wife tapped the shopping cart.

I lowered my eyes. "Sorry." I put my hand over my mouth through the next aisle.

Then my wife announced, "We need to get both kids a compass for math."

I couldn't help myself. "We don't need to spend money on that, do we? Did you ever use your compass more than once when you were in school? My compass just sat in my desk the whole year. And every time I reached in there to grab something, I pricked my fingers on the stupid thing."

"*Ken!*"

"And I wasn't the only one," I added. "When the teacher said to take out a book or piece of paper, all over the classroom, kids would be rolling on the floor in pain."

My wife didn't look amused. "The list says to bring a compass. So we are bringing a compass."

"All right, but we'd better stop and get Band-Aids too."

A couple of minutes later, my son came around the corner. "Here's the boxes of Kleenex."

"*Kleenex?*" I shouted. "The kids use their sleeves. Have you ever seen them actually use a Kleenex?"

A salesclerk poked her head around the corner. "Can I help you folks?"

My wife pointed at me. "He needs some help."

While I was asking the clerk where to find the used school supplies, my family ditched me.

They say every child in this country gets a free education. They lie.

REFLECTION

I'm jealous of Job. (And yes, I know that's one more sin to add to the list.) Where does a guy get faith like that to handle such horrific happenings in his life? My trip to the mall pales in comparison, and yet I can't handle even that.

Before I had children, I seriously thought I had the patience of Job. Really. I did. On a spectrum of 1 to 10, I'd have rated myself an 11. Once I had children, I realized I am roughly a 1.45.

Children challenge us—there is no escaping that. The truth is, life can be hard.

Here's what Paul says: "And not only so, but we glory in tribulations also: knowing that tribulation worketh patience" (Rom. 5:3 KJV).

There it is again. We suffer to be closer to God.

We suffer to be closer to God.

It is equally true, however, that life is joyous, fun, and beautiful. Which begs the question, how often do I say, "Life is fun"? How often do I thank God for an amazing day? And how does that compare to all the times I look to heaven and exclaim, "Why me, God?"

Did I ever model gratitude to my children, or was I just always harping on them to be grateful? I'll bet Job noticed the good times in his life.

I am pretty certain that God wants me to be patient. I'm tempted to say that patience equals faith. At the very least, both are on Paul's list of the fruit of the Spirit (see Gal. 5:22–25). And that is an important lesson for us all. Questioning the work that God is mysteriously doing in my life is another way of losing patience with Him.

> **Questioning the work that God is mysteriously doing in my life is another way of losing patience with Him.**

Of course He is there for me. And the challenges He throws my way in my roles as father and husband are perfectly orchestrated for me and my family's benefit. I could certainly do less complaining and be more reflective. If I listened more carefully, I'd probably be a lot more tolerant, as well as more grateful.

If there is one thing I could recommend, it would be to do a year of gratefulness work. A book for that is *Simple Abundance* by Sarah Ban Breathnach. It will change your life.

Verse: "This is the day that the LORD has made; let us rejoice and be glad in it" (Ps. 118:24 ESV).

Further Reading:

> Book of Job
> Psalm 103
> Matthew 6

Prayer: Saying out loud five things I am grateful for today, every day, brings me closer to You, Lord. Instill in me the habit of this venture to glorify You, and forever change my outlook. I am a better person when I focus on the gifts You provide me. From birdsong to baby babble, I am surrounded by goodness always, and in this I am truly blessed. Amen.

CHAPTER EIGHT

Cleanliness Is Next to Godliness

I brought the children into my den for a difficult discussion.

"Kids, it's about your mom." My voice sounded rattled and on edge. "There's something you should know. It's not going to be easy to hear."

Deep down inside, the children must have been dreading what I was about to say. They looked scared.

"So, it's true?" my son asked, the color gone from his face. "It has really come to this?"

"Yes," I replied. "Your mom refuses to pick up after us anymore."

It was almost too painful to even say.

My son walked to the window and stared outside quietly. My daughter wept.

We'd always known my wife liked a tidy, neat, perfectly ordered house. But I started to suspect something was wrong a few weeks before this discussion when I found her standing in the middle of the cluttered family room, crying. She said she was at the end of her rope. She explained that she had tried everything she could think of to inspire us to pick up after ourselves … yelling, hiding our things, and now crying.

I gave her a hug and told her it was okay—that the kids and I didn't mind the mess.

Lesson 1: Don't say that to a clean freak.

In retaliation, my wife conducted a secret experiment on us. She didn't clean up after the children and me for a solid week so that we could see what slobs we were. She said it was the hardest thing she'd ever had to do. Then, when the kids and I didn't notice, she went to plan B: mopping the floors with our clothes.

I finally agreed to change after her plan C: refusing to wash our underwear.

That's when I convened the meeting with the children.

"So, kids, as you can see, your mother has proven that she's not only frustrated with how messy things are, but she's also not above hanging our unmentionables from the flagpole."

My daughter wiped her eyes. "Do you think Grandma would come live here and pick up after us?"

"Sure," I said. "How do you feel about your mom having her own apartment?"

She shrugged.

"Look, I know this is unpleasant," I told them, "but I think we must face facts here."

My son nodded. "Yep. We need to hire a maid."

"No," I retorted. "I was thinking that you should go pick up your backpacks in the living room. I'll remove my ice cream bowl from under the couch. And whoever walked in the house with their shoes on better get a broom and sweep. Okay?"

The children nodded and ran from the room.

The next second, my wife walked into the den. "What was that all about?"

"Don't worry, honey. I took care of the problem," I said proudly. "After quite a long and compelling meeting, I can safely say that the kids have agreed to start picking up after themselves."

"And they're happy about that?"

"Of course," I lied.

"Really?" she asked, pointing out the window. "So why are they running away down the street?"

I hoped to round up the kids before my wife devised a plan D, but I was too slow. "I have a new plan," she said a couple of days later. "Each week, each of you owes me one solid hour to do whatever it is that I want you to do."

I blushed. "Honey, not in front of the children."

Lesson 2: Don't make jokes in a situation like this.

Needless to say, we didn't take her new plan to heart. So, she went to plan E: burning our dinner.

That's when I convened a meeting with the children on the front stoop.

"So, kids, as you can see, your mother has proven that she's not only frustrated with how chores aren't getting done around here, but she's also not above locking us out of the house."

My daughter wiped her eyes. "If we agree to her plan, do you think she'll let us back in?"

My son nodded. "Before the sprinklers come back on?"

Once we put it in writing, we did in fact get let back into the house. And our first chore was wiping our face smudges off the windows.

In the weeks to come, we cleaned out the garage, put a new shelving system into the pantry, power-washed the driveway, painted the trim on the house, and swept out behind the refrigerator. It was a huge success ... in my wife's mind.

Was Mary so patient that she never harped on Joseph to pick up his dirty socks and cereal bowl in the living room?

My wife gave me a new job once—the laundry.

I'd never taken on laundry in our many years of chores ... I mean, *marriage*. I'd had plenty of other duties, like cleaning toilets and washing dishes—you know, the easy stuff. I had no idea how great I'd had it.

I don't know how it is at your house, but my family appeared to be involved in a twenty-four-hour opera with twenty-seven costume changes a day ... and I had become the poor slob in charge of the washing. It was a monstrous job with absolutely no end in sight.

Case in point: You know how they say to separate the loads? Putting the reds with the reds, the darks with the darks, and so forth? I would've needed a backhoe to do that.

Towels were the worst. At any given moment, there was an average of eighteen soggy bath towels, eight damp hand towels, thirteen wrinkled washcloths, seven wet beach towels, twenty-one sopping kitchen towels, and two clammy pot holders waiting for me to come home and break my back lifting them into the washing machine. And I had just caught up the previous weekend.

How could a family go through that many towels? We weren't that clean.

Finally, I had to ask the kids what was going on.

"Kids, after school, when Daddy is at work, are you showering the homeless?"

What else could account for the amount of laundry that stacked up in my laundry room?

Well, *stacked* may not be the right term. I stacked the laundry. My wife stacked the laundry. My children tossed the laundry from their rooms hoping it would land on the stacked laundry. They couldn't throw.

Once, I walked into the house and wondered how a twister had touched down in the laundry room. I didn't know funnel clouds could form on a ceiling. I'd never seen so many clothes strewn in so many directions. I did the only thing humanly possible: I went to bed.

I know I shouldn't have complained, seeing as my wife had done this horrible, terrible job for our entire marriage. And believe me when I say this, she had no sympathy for me. In fact, one day while I was sobbing into a dryer sheet, she did a little victory dance all the way down the hall.

Of course, my biggest fear was that when it came time to switch jobs again, there would be nothing I could offer to entice my wife to take back the laundry duty. I realized I could quite possibly be stuck shoveling clothes for the next several decades—if, that was, I wasn't killed in an avalanche of whites first.

One day, a friend came over and stated the obvious. "The problem is that you haven't enlisted your teenagers in the task—sought their buy-in and given them the responsibility of the job. If they are creating most of the laundry, then shouldn't they be in charge of handling the problem?"

Oh, we'd tried giving our teenagers the job of laundry. Here's how the conversation between my wife and me went on the last day of that experiment.

> Me: (exasperated) Why don't any of our socks match?
>
> My wife: Your son was in charge of folding the laundry this week.
>
> Me: (exhausted) Why are our shirts a combination of pink and blue?
>
> My wife: Your daughter was in charge of separating the laundry this week.
>
> Me: Why do we have to go out in public with shirts and pants that look like they've been trampled by wolves?
>
> My wife: The children fought over whose turn it was to transfer the clothes from the washer to the dryer this week.
>
> Me: How can you be so calm about all this?
>
> My wife: I'm pretending I'm shipwrecked on a deserted island with a suitcase belonging to a hobo.
>
> Me: Does that help?
>
> My wife: As long as I pretend I'm intoxicated.

Don't get me wrong: my wife and I firmly believe that children should be given responsibilities and chores around the house so they not only learn the value of hard work but also see that being part of a family means chipping in and sharing part of the load—in good times and in bad. We tried to instill those values as often as we could.

There is, however, one thing also to keep in mind. It's not always prudent to pick chores for children without first giving thought to the consequences. Especially when that particular chore carries the risk that one day, when you least expect it, you'll undress at the Y and your skivvies will be pink.

REFLECTION

The phrase *cleanliness is next to godliness* jumps quickly to mind after these two stories. That phrase doesn't actually exist in the Bible. However, scholars suggest that Psalm 19:9 might be the genesis of the idea: "The fear of the LORD is clean, enduring forever; the rules of the LORD are true, and righteous altogether" (ESV).

As discussed in chapter 4, there's purity not only in a mother's love for her family but also in her desire to create a "clean" environment for us. Moms worry about stuff like that, I believe, because they feel a calling from God to accommodate, serve, protect, and prepare—even if maybe they wouldn't describe it that way.

It's easy to take my wife for granted. I love her and I try to be considerate, but I fall short time after time. I think I take Mary, Jesus' mom, for granted too. We should thank God more often for the works she did on earth—bearing and raising our Savior, Jesus Christ. We should aspire to the faith she had in God. Certainly, her "fear" of God was both clean and pure.

Incidentally, we should thank our wives and moms, too, for supporting us and the children. That's no small matter.

If I did that, maybe I'd have fewer conversations like the following.

"Where are my shoes?" I asked my wife, staring dumbfoundedly at the place in the kitchen where I'd left them only moments ago.

"I put them away."

"I just got them out."

"Oh."

My wife is a compulsive picker-upper. She moves steadily throughout the house like a minesweeper picking up things and putting them away. Only, it doesn't matter how long the items have been there.

I barely hold on to anything. If I turn my back or put something down for a moment—*whoosh*, it's gone. You name it:

Half a glass of water—it's in the dishwasher.

A half-read newspaper—into the recycle bin.

Half a cookie—grabbed off my plate.

"Hey! I was eating that!"

"You looked like you were finished."

"I was chewing."

Granted, the kids were messy—and I continue to be messy. My wife says she does it to stay on top of the chores. But I think it's more than that. It's become an obsession.

She can't stand even a small mess or anything past its prime.

In our house, you won't find mold on our cheese, milk a day past its carton date, or confetti a minute after midnight. Flowers barely bloom before they're tossed onto the compost pile.

I've spent hours hunting around an area where I've left something for "just" a couple of minutes, only later to discover the item has been packed away in the attic or given to Goodwill. I have to think twice before laying something down. The last thing I want to see is the garbage man standing at the curb reviewing my latest prostate exam.

Frankly, it frightens me a little bit. I told my wife this once.

"Honey, I've never said this out loud before, but I'm afraid to get old and feeble. I'm worried you'll tidy up and put *me* someplace, like a closet or a drawer, and I'll be stuck there forever."

The kids used to try to keep up with her, but even they were usually too slow to react. They had toys disappear, Halloween candy vanish, dirty shirts ripped off their bodies.

Jack cornered me once. "We have to do something about Mom."

"Why?" I asked.

"Because, a few minutes ago, I blew a bubble and left it hanging out of my mouth a second too long."

I gasped. "Mom reached out and took your gum?"

"Yes—and a loose tooth with it. See?"

It's not that I didn't appreciate what my wife was trying to do. I knew the kids and I weren't easy to live with, and I did enjoy the fact that our place looked orderly and clean. She did an exemplary job of running a tight ship. She made sure that everything we owned had a rightful place. She truly was doing God's work.

I'm a lucky man.

It's just that I don't know where she put my notes so I can finish this chapter. I put them down for only a second. I was going to include a great section on … Oh well, never mind.

Verse: "The angel went to her and said, 'Greetings, you who are highly favored! The Lord is with you'" (Luke 1:28).

Further Reading:

> Isaiah 7:14
> Luke 1
> John 2

Prayer: Holy Father, I am eternally grateful for the women in my life. Please continue to bless them, and help me express my gratitude to them often. I pray that all my children will find special women to guide them as wives, mothers-in-law, sisters-in-law, and more. Thank You for Mary as well, for the living examples of faith, love, and devotion she gave us all. Amen.

CHAPTER NINE

Feel the Burn

Are your children affecting your health and fitness? Did the gym recently call wondering if you'd died because they haven't seen you in a couple of years? Do you feel you're losing the battle of the bulge? Do you have the sneaking suspicion that your role as a busy parent may be affecting your time to stay fit and trim? Find out where you stand with this test developed in my lab at home.

1. Stress Relief. Reducing tension is one of the major contributing factors for good health and fitness. How do you rejuvenate your spirit during the day?

> a. I visit a massage therapist three days a week to work the stress of children out of my body.
> b. I play soft music in my car and at home while I drink soothing tea.
> c. I run errands all day, and then I sleep through parent conferences with my eyes open.

2. Exercise. Experts contend that the best way to lose weight is to eat less and exercise more. What's your exercise routine?

a. I jog every day while the kids are at preschool.

b. I always take the stairs, and I do yoga for fifteen minutes before bedtime.

c. I work my upper body by carrying thirty pounds of supplies to the daycare center every morning, then I get a good thigh workout trying to leave with my sobbing son wrapped around my ankle like a leg weight.

3. Nutrition. Eating healthy is key. Describe your average meal at work.

a. I pack my own lunch with sensible, low-fat, organic foods that I mindfully prepare with the perfect element of chi.

b. I eat lunch at the corner health-food store and chew each bite twenty-seven times.

c. I'm lucky if I have time to grab one of the kids' Lunchables from the fridge before rushing out of the house. If that doesn't work, I pray it is someone's birthday in the office so I can at least eat a piece of cake.

4. Sleep. Nothing affects your health and stamina more than a good night's sleep. What's your typical night like?

a. I go to bed early so I am refreshed and energetic all day long.

b. I get the standard eight hours of sleep.

c. I wander from room to room all night nursing babies, changing wet sheets, and comforting sick children. Then I drink six cups of coffee in the morning to wake up and hope I leave the house with matching shoes.

5. Me Time. Spending time alone doing the things you enjoy cuts down on those awful feelings of resentment and, in the end, makes for a happier, better-adjusted you. What kind of "me time" do you get?

a. I schedule plenty of spa treatments, quiet meals, and long walks.

b. I say no to people, and I never bite off more than I can chew—thus leaving lots of time for myself to reinvigorate.

c. I want to take my overstuffed day planner and maim people who answered *a* or *b*.

6. Fluids. Researchers say that drinking lots of water results in a healthier body. How many fluids do you get?

a. I drink eight glasses a day.

b. I drink six glasses a day.

c. I stick out my tongue and catch the tears as they roll off my exhausted face.

YOUR SCORE

Now, tally up your scores. Give yourself 10 points for every time you answered *a*, 5 points for every *b* answer, and 1 point for a *c* response.

If you scored 50 points or more, you can expect to live until you're 100 years old.

If you scored over 20 points, you are what doctors consider a healthy, well-adjusted person.

If your score was below 20 points, you may need to lose 20 pounds … and pray … a lot!

I'm not proud of it, but the sin I turned to more often than not to counterbalance the pressures and stresses of parenthood was … drum roll … gluttony. When I was younger, no one would have known this because I had the metabolism of a stick bug. But after turning 40, I became a walking advertisement for Jenny Craig.

And so did my wife (but don't tell her I wrote that). We were codependents in our sin of gluttony, which sometimes led to conversations like this one:

"I need a new weight-loss plan," my wife announced.

Pause.

"Ken, why aren't you saying anything?"

"I'm holding my breath."

She frowned. "Don't you want to know what my new plan is?"

I shook my head.

"I am hiring help," she said.

"Are you getting a personal trainer?" I asked.

"No."

"Dietician?"

"No."

I cringed. "You aren't paying a doctor to remove your sweat glands, are you?"

"No."

"Then who is helping you?"

"You."

I accidentally swallowed my gum. "Not again."

"Yes, I want you to help me!" she exclaimed. "I want your support."

"You want me to be your food cop, don't you? You want me to keep you from overeating?"

"Yes."

I hated that job. I had a hard enough time managing my own gluttony. Sure, it may sound like a reasonable request—me reminding her of her dietary goals. But what she really wanted me to do was literally remove the food from her hands and/or say mean things like "Drop that fruit pie, honey, before all you can wear is a Hefty bag!"

What's especially bad about that was while she wanted me to be her diet policeman, she also bit my head off when I performed these duties.

"I don't want the job," I told her.

"Why not?"

"Because last time you called me names."

"I did not. Like what?"

I cocked my head. "You called me an insensitive, miserable, hard-to-please poopie head."

She waved me off. "That's because you made piggy noises every time I opened the refrigerator."

"You told me to do that!"

"I know—I thought you'd be able to handle the pressure. You want to support me, don't you?"

I sat down. "Let me get this straight. You want me to be harsh with you, but I'm not supposed to be offended when you criticize me for being a jerk, even though you want me to really be a jerk?"

She nodded.

"And if you cry when I make the swine noises, what am I supposed to do?"

"Duck."

See what I mean? It's a no-win situation for me.

"So where did you get the idea that I should say these mean things to you?" I asked.

"From this," she said holding up a book by Dr. Sheila Gunderson titled *You Eat Like a Hippo.*

"That doesn't sound nice!" I exclaimed.

"Look, if I wanted nice, I'd call my mom so she can tell me *again* that my double chin is a sign of sincerity."

I sighed. "All right, I'll try. But what about the other problem?"

"What other problem?"

"About having to say these mean things to you in public," I answered. "Let's just say I've noticed that other women don't appreciate it when we are at a party and they hear me telling you to spit out the cream puff."

"Why? Did someone say something to you?"

"No, but when I'm not looking, they knock my drinks over."

Not that any of this makes the actual exercise process any less strenuous.

Years ago, I did yoga in a hot, 105-degree room with my wife.

Known as Hot Box Yoga (or Hot Sweaty Yoga or I'm Going to Pass Out Yoga), it involved spending ninety minutes performing various postures in a heated studio—sort of like stretching in a sauna but you get to wear more than just a towel … barely.

One yoga studio's website describes it this way: "This extreme temperature warms and helps relax the muscles and causes excessive sweating, which followers claim flushes toxins from the body."

I can't say for sure that I released any toxins when I participated, but I can confirm that hot, sweaty yoga made my shorts stick to my bottom like cellophane.

I also learned it's important not to wear white.

I still remember my first class, the previous fall. My wife asked if I wanted to do hot yoga, and I said sure … thinking it was yoga with supermodels. Little did I know that the only panting I'd be doing would be due to dehydration.

In the first five minutes, I was literally a sweaty mess. And not just because the room was unbearably hot. Believe it or not, standing on your tippy toes and at the same time sitting down on an invisible chair can make you sweat … and want to scream. "Scream and Sweat"—that's what I'd call my hot yoga studio.

I am told these yoga poses ultimately make participants more relaxed in their lives. I am also told that the CIA uses these same techniques when trying to get information out of prisoners.

There are customs to know before joining a hot, sweaty yoga program. During a class, for example, participants are asked not to talk so that others can stay focused on their practice. Of course, I think the real reason behind the rule is to keep husbands from turning to their wives and saying, "Thanks for bringing me, honey—I've always wanted an exercise program that makes me feel like throwing up."

After completing fifteen of these classes, though I hated to admit it, I was feeling more relaxed, more flexible, and less nauseated. I wasn't ready to bend like a pretzel or anything, but I was able to stop taking Dramamine before each class.

Even today, I am excited to find out the next experience my wife has planned for us. Maybe we'll try biking, hiking, or shaving off our fat with Chinese throwing knives. Regardless, I bet it will be relaxing.

I also recently joined a gym to do weightlifting.

After my first workout, I came home and told my wife how it went.

"Honey, I think I was quite the inspiration today."

She smiled. "Because you were all studly?"

"No, because the other people working out now have a better idea what happens to the human body when it's left to rot."

She said it couldn't be that bad. I told her I was surprised no one asked to take my picture so they could tape it to their bathroom mirror as motivation.

Frankly, it stinks to be the weakest guy at the gym—huffing and puffing my way around, breaking a sweat in the locker room as I put my shoes on. There's nothing worse than being the weakest guy at the gym. Except, of course, being the weakest guy at the gym while being lapped on the indoor track by the Lite & Lively Stroke Survivors class.

Still, I suppose, I had to start somewhere.

My wife said she was proud that at least I was trying. I told her I would hold on to that thought the next time I was doing push-ups … with my knees on the ground.

After my first day at the gym, I regrouped. I reminded myself of the health benefits and returned happily the next day. After my lunchtime workout, I called my wife at work.

"Did it go better today?" she asked.

"Kind of," I told her. "But when I wasn't looking, someone put a blue handicapped parking sign on the handlebars of my stationary bike."

"That wasn't nice," she replied. "Did anyone stop to help you?"

"One person was kind enough to hold the bike steady for me as I climbed off," I said.

"Well, that was nice of him."

"You mean her."

"Her?"

"Yes, an elderly lady from the Jazzercise class helped me down."

"Did she say anything to you?"

"No, but I could see the questions forming on her face."

"Questions?" my wife asked. "Like what?"

"Oh, questions like 'Sir, exactly how many years were you in the coma?'"

The next day, I drove by the gym five times before finally talking myself into going inside. I changed quickly, and then I decided to give the free-weight room a try. I called my wife this time from my cell phone.

"Honey," I said, "if you get the chance, would you call someone to come down here and get this barbell off my chest?"

She admonished me for pushing the envelope and going straight to the free weights. She said I needed to be more careful and remember that getting into shape is a process that takes time and commitment. I thanked her for her advice, and then I reminded her that the barbell was crushing my ribs.

Oof!

REFLECTION

I know shoving food into my face is not God's plan for me. In many ways, it is disrespectful to treat the body He gave me as poorly as I do. But I also know that trying to slim down for the sin of pride, to look good for others, doesn't serve me well either. Too often, I have promised myself to get into better shape for no other reason than to stop looking like the "before" picture in a weight-loss ad.

There's something much deeper to discover as I put down the cookies and strengthen my body. I'm not describing self-flagellation or fasting. I'm talking about respect. I *try* to remind myself that I was created in His image, which is pure perfection. I think that means He loves me no matter how I look, and I owe it to myself to show gratitude for my perfect self by taking care of my mind and body.

I also try not to beat myself up when I don't do this.

Staying connected with God through prayer and conversation helps me stay motivated too. I am not saying I am good at this, but in those few times when I experience the good vibrations of being in God's presence, I am at true peace. The more I do that, the less I turn to gluttony and other sins. And once in that place of balance, I can get off the couch and do something good for me.

How do I connect with God? Practice. Tons of it! I make space in my day to rest for a few minutes, to turn off my mind and feel His presence in my body. When I find Him there, I pray for His support and love.

Just like everything else, it is a habit I continue to practice.

Verse: "Do you not know that your bodies are temples of the Holy Spirit, who is in you, whom you have received from God? You are not your own; you were bought at a price. Therefore honor God with your bodies" (1 Cor. 6:19–20).

Further Reading:

> Genesis 1
> Romans 12
> 1 Corinthians 3

Prayer: Lord, today, I pledge to treat my body with the respect due to You for creating me in Your own image. The greatest gift was bestowed upon me, and I owe it to You, Lord, and to myself to honor both my mind and my body. I am also beholden to my family, and it is my responsibility to be here to mentor, protect, and love them as well. When I take care of myself, I show my respect and devotion to all who rely on me. Help me, Lord, to avoid the temptations that keep me from this purpose. Amen.

CHAPTER TEN

Casting Stones

Years ago, a client George had never met in person invited his family to dinner. When they arrived at the house, George discovered that his client was missing his right hand.

Now George's son, Jess, who was seven years old at the time, had never seen anyone who was missing a body part. Needless to say, during the entire dinner, Jess sat mesmerized, staring at the hook that replaced the man's right hand. So transfixed he was that, several times, George had to lean over to Jess and tell him to close his mouth.

Finally, George's client decided to give Jess a break. He leaned toward the youngster and said, "Jess, it's okay. You can ask me the question that is on your mind."

"Really?" Jess replied.

"Sure," the man said. "Believe me, I get asked this question a lot."

Glancing at his dad, Jess looked for George's okay to proceed. George gave an encouraging nod.

Confident, Jess turned to the man with the missing hand and asked, "So, exactly how *do* you wipe your bum?"

Silence.

Now it was George's turn to sit there with his mouth agape. Obviously, everyone at the table had thought Jess would ask how the man had lost his hand. But that would've been too easy.

As parents, most of us have found ourselves in embarrassing moments, thanks to our children. One of these for me was way back in 1997, when my daughter was a kindergartner. It was a Friday, which meant only one thing in that kindergarten—show-and-tell.

My daughter had her mind set all week on bringing her Hula Hair Barbie to show-and-tell. She had the doll, which was dressed in a grass skirt and bikini top made out of coconuts, sitting by the front door for days in anticipation of the big day.

For those who can't remember show-and-tell, most teachers use the tradition as a way to teach communication skills. Children stand up and, in a clear and confident tone, run down the features of the item they brought from home like excited car salesmen giving the specs on a race car. Meanwhile, the other children in the room, who literally are almost peeing their pants they are so excited to present their own products, are learning not only how to sit patiently and listen but also how to raise their hands and articulate questions for the presenter.

When it was my daughter's turn to give her glorious highlights of living with Hula Hair Barbie, she walked like a queen to the front of the class, pulled Barbie out from behind her back, and held up the Polynesian beauty as if it were the Hope Diamond.

After her presentation, it was time for the other children to ask pertinent questions about Hula Hair Barbie. Glancing around the room, my daughter lifted her arm and pointed to another little girl in the front, offering that child the good fortune to address not only my daughter but also Hula Hair Barbie.

The little girl cleared her throat and asked, "What do you like best about Hula Hair Barbie?"

"That's easy," my sweet, little, innocent child replied. To demonstrate, my daughter reached up, ripped off Barbie's coconut bikini top, pointed at the plastic bumps, and said, "Oh, I like these!"

That was the year I was PTA president of the school.

To be a parent takes a lot of humility.

To be a parent takes a lot of humility.

Especially when the kids are gone and the phone rings. I got "the call" one long-ago summer. The kind that starts with the person on the other end of the phone line asking if I was Mr. Swarner and ends with the sentence "Could you please come pick up your children? They're causing problems."

The lifeguard of our community pool sounded exasperated as he said that.

A thousand questions flashed across my mind—my mouth could barely catch up: "What did my kids do? Were they told not to do it before they did it? What are they doing right now? Would you mind holding the line for a moment while I die from embarrassment?"

I assured the lifeguard I would be there right away, especially after he told me my boys had thrown pool chairs at each other.

All excuses aside, calls like these are humiliating.

The moment I stepped out of my house, I sensed a hundred eyes staring at me, as if the entire neighborhood had already heard news reports of the incident.

> Radio Announcer: This just in, Ken Swarner's children are in hot water following a fight at the community pool. Sources say Michael Swarner, 14, threw a plastic chair at his little brother, Jack, 11. Ken Swarner is reportedly en route to the scene of the altercation. Unconfirmed reports say he has been spotted screaming inside his car and pounding his head on the steering wheel.

As I pulled up to the pool, I scanned the parking lot to see if I recognized any of the other parents' cars. Parents, mind you, who were supervising their children at the pool. Sure, all their kids were under nine years old, but it didn't negate the fact that my kids had fought a war with each other using lawn furniture.

I could feel these moms and dads staring at me from their chairs as I marched up to the lifeguard. Luckily for me, the guard recounted the entire incident … loudly. I am sure those who had arrived late appreciated the recap.

To top it off, I got a parenting lecture from this seventeen-year-old.

"I told your kids that they may be able to act that way at home but not here," the pimple-faced lifeguard explained.

I let out a small chuckle in order to suppress the hundred sarcastic quips I had on the tip of my tongue. I am sure the laughter didn't further my case. I tried to recover by explaining that my wife and I didn't tolerate such behavior from our kids. I was about to also say, "We certainly don't act this way at home," when my youngest shouted, *"Dad, it's like that time Michael threw the hamper at me!"*

I made each child apologize to the guard, and then I turned to usher my children toward the parking lot. Unfortunately, curiosity got the better of me, and I looked up for a second to see who had witnessed the debacle. My eyes locked with my son's den mother. I shrugged, smiled, and said weakly to her, "Kids will be kids," just as her son snapped his candy bar and handed half to his sister.

Then there was the time when, while I was away on business, my wife took our daughter and our daughter's best friend to church. My wife sang in the church choir, which meant that our children had to sit by themselves during the service.

They had done this before without incident. However, for some reason (still not exactly clear), my daughter and her friend decided that week to sit in the front pew rather than where we normally sit, near the back. At our church, the seating faces the front in a half circle. Therefore, the girls were at center stage.

It went without saying that in the Swarner family, we always behaved in church. That was why, one Sunday years ago, it came as a shock to my wife when the choir member to her left leaned over and told her that she might want to direct her attention to the center row seating.

As the priest was moving up and down the aisles, sprinkling the parishioners with the Holy Waters of Baptism, my daughter and her friend were leaned completely over in their pew, with their heads facing the floor, combing their dangling, long hair with their fingers. Every so often, they'd flip their heads back, sending hair flying in tumultuous waves, then hunch back over to continue their holy primping.

I don't know about you, but we tend to frown on such behavior in our church. I mean, there isn't anything handed down by the pope on the subject, but when the father says, "Let us pray," it's really no time to be examining split ends.

But wait … it gets worse.

After the collection, when it was time to kneel, my daughter, who (you'll remember) was in the front row where there wasn't a kneeling bar or even a partition between her and the altar, got down on her knees, arched her back all prim and proper, and then folded her hands in a pious-like (see *theatrical*, or better yet, *goofball*) manner.

Apparently, in my daughter's mind, what Jesus would do was mock the holy rite of Communion.

My poor wife sat trapped in the choir section, helpless to do anything other than throw darts with her eyes at our daughter.

If I had been there, I don't know if the apparent smirk on my daughter's face at the time would have been the crowning moment for me or if that would have come later when my daughter lost her balance and fell to the floor. It doesn't really matter. I'm sure either reason would have given me a coronary.

My daughter had no explanation whatsoever for her behavior, which gave my wife little to go on when three parishioners stopped her and expressed their disappointment after the Mass.

These parishioners weren't single people, or for that matter married folks without children. They weren't nuns, or more importantly, not even the priest. Instead, these were fellow parents—comrades in arms—people who had children of their own.

Talk about a trio of Judases.

The most audacious mom to approach had raised four boys of her own. With a sour look on her face, she asked my wife, "Would it be okay if I talked to your daughter and explained the proper way to act in church?"

For the new parents out there, that's code for "Obviously you can't be trusted to parent the child—maybe I should do it for you."

Next, she told my wife, "You shouldn't be embarrassed. It's not your fault your daughter acted that way in church today."

Which is code for "You should be humiliated."

I can't imagine doing that to another parent, for three reasons.

> 1. Unless the unruly child's parents were clapping, shouting "Bravo," or calling aunts and uncles on their cell phones from the pew to brag about their child's behavior, I'd assume that the parents were already formulating ways to address the situation on their own. Not to mention planning to place extra cash in the church collection basket the next week.
> 2. If it wasn't my child, I'd most likely be thanking God it wasn't me.
> 3. I might as well take out my calendar and set the date and time for my child to act inappropriately in public the minute I condemn another person's child.

My wife shrugged the woman off but later fumed. When I got home, she and I did all the classic things people do when an incident like this happens:

1. Acted indignant and hurt.

2. Spent hours telling the "demeaning" story to friends and family.

3. Listed all the "bad" things the busybodies had done in the past.

4. Ate a whole cheesecake.

In fact, we were so caught up in the drama that it was nearly bedtime before we realized we had forgotten to address our daughter about her behavior in church.

That surely took the wind out of our sails.

I suppose it's also appropriate that this happened at church. After all, in God's house, He's used to hearing people ask, "Oh, Lord, why me?"

I loved watching old TV shows growing up. I watched episodes of *The Brady Bunch*, *Happy Days*, and *Leave It to Beaver*. One of the characteristics these families all shared was that the Bradys, Cunninghams, and Cleavers ate dinner together ... happily ... with the children. At the table, the kids calmly discussed the day's events while politely passing the potatoes. They placed their napkins in their clean laps and sat still. They asked permission (yes, asked) to leave the table when they were finished and then (brace yourself) took their dirty dishes to the sink. I think a couple of times they even said, "Thank you."

Why does this spoil my appetite now?

Because those TV families led me to believe that this was normal … they acted as if there was nothing special about their heavenly mealtimes, and they made me think that I'd share this same experience when I became a father.

Boy, had the tables turned.

Eating with my children was like dining with Vikings. There was Eirikr the Wolfer, Gandalfr the Grabber, Balasar the Interrupter, and Queen Rannveig of the Open Mouth Chewers.

There wasn't a meal that went by that one child didn't say something disgusting, talk with bread crumbs shooting out his or her mouth like confetti, or ask me to pull a finger. If they designed a television show about my family at the dinner table, it would be called *Dad's about to Have an Aneurysm*.

I might have been better prepared for my own disastrous dining experiences had those subversive TV families from my youth been more like my own. I would have had lower expectations of my kids' eating habits if, possibly, I had seen Peter Brady serve himself salad with his hands. I probably wouldn't have felt a painful twinge of guilt at the sound of "Dinner's ready" if in at least one episode Joanie Cunningham had rhymed each item on the table with a potty word as she passed it to Mr. C. I might even have had a little peace of mind if just once, *just once*, Wally Cleaver had teased his naive little brother, Beaver, into thinking that tonight's meat loaf was actually their cat, Muffin.

If only my world hadn't been painted so rosy with a deceitful basting brush.

So, with that all said, you can better understand my state of mind when I once looked across the noisy dinner table at my wife (as one child was under the table) and exclaimed, "Honey, guess what? I'm thinking about getting my own apartment!"

She asked me to take her with me.

It's not that I gave up working to improve their manners. I even tried to get my kids interested in the same television programs I watched as a kid. I sat them down in front of TV Land and pointed out the Beave's excellent etiquette, Cindy Brady's superb dish-passing skills, and Richie Cunningham's well-received compliments to the chef. They laughed so hard the dog hid in the upstairs closet.

My biggest concern, though, wasn't the pillaging going on at my own house. I was most worried whenever a child of mine got invited to eat at someone else's house. I just hated the thought that a parent would be sitting around his or her own table, watching in horror as my Viking child pounded through three helpings, worried that once the food ran out things could get dicey.

In other words, I was worried about being judged.

In other words, I was worried

about being judged.

My children assured me they knew how to behave when they were in other people's homes. They said they didn't eat like barbarians anywhere else but at our own dinner table.

I guess they meant one of three things:

1. They felt comfortable to be themselves at my dinner table.

2. They didn't want to embarrass their parents in public.

3. They hated their mother and me.

Some experts contend that more and more modern-day families are no longer eating meals together like they once did.

I can't blame them.

Humiliation leads to all sorts of insecurities raising children. It led to me wishing that there was a support group for parents who have a child who brings home a grade lower than a C. They could meet once a week in an unmarked location. It could be a place where they could freely share their frustrations ... get advice ... hug.

I never got a grade lower than a C in school. And I certainly never thought my own child would do something like that ... until my son's report card appeared.

I can't even write what the grades were. Not without banging my head on the keyboard.

I know I shouldn't be, especially after so much time has passed, but I am embarrassed by his poor grades. I would hear other parents bragging about their children's great marks, and I couldn't help but wonder what was wrong with me. Where had my wife and I gone wrong? How could we have done a better job instilling the love of education? How had we failed our son?

Luckily, most parents don't ask about another child's grades—at least, they didn't back then. They would just tell me about how great their own kids were doing in school. Still, there was always that uncomfortable silence when they were done, as if it was now my turn to brag about my children's grades.

I usually took that time to point out that my son recently had a successful dentist appointment, just to make myself feel better.

"The dentist gave him an A for gums and a B+ for tartar. I'm beside myself." (In truth, that's a lie. The dentist asked if we could find time to attend his Good Brushing class as a family.)

I suppose I could've forced my son to get better marks in school. He was an extremely bright, gifted child. It would've just been a matter of me standing over him each evening, putting the pencil in his hand, and moving his arm across the paper. My only concern was what would happen when he passed these classes and then went off to college. Would I have to go too? Would I be the oldest guy in the fraternity?

"Panty-raid time, Mr. Swarner!"

"Dudes! I'll be there after my son and I finish his term paper. Put that pencil back in your hand, son!"

I wasn't asking for my son to get perfect scores. Average, I guess, would have been fine.

My wife liked to say that it was our son's lesson to learn. She contended that it was *his* future that lay in the balance. It was his consequence to face if he passed or failed school. She said it didn't reflect poorly on us when he simply refused to do the work.

I suppose she was right. If he flunked school, was unable to get a good job, and lived on the streets, maybe he'd finally see how important an education is.

Of course, while homelessness would probably be a good lesson for him, my annual Christmas letter was going to be a challenge. What would I write?

"Season's Greetings. It's been another busy year at the Swarner house. I published a book this year. Allison performed beautifully in the church choir. Our daughter, Claire, finished her first year of college. And our son ate out of a garbage can. Happy Holidays."

That's going to be embarrassing!

REFLECTION

It's moments like these that can teach us humility ... as if that's a lesson anyone really wants to learn. Like it or not, however, such incidents are the cornerstones not only of being a child of God but also of being a parent of a child. (If that's *not* true for you, please keep it to yourself.)

Ironically, my pride gets in the way of me learning humility. The casting of stones in these anecdotes didn't come from others ... they came from inside me. I was the one judging myself— hurting myself. Even in the incident at church with my daughter, those comments from a fellow parishioner hurt ... because of my lack of humility. The proper course would have been to feel emboldened to teach my daughter the errors of her decision, say a quiet prayer for the mom judging us, and understand that what happened, well, happens. Instead, I chose indignation.

That's hard to swallow, but it is true. If we are not humbled before God, then we allow ego and pride to take over, which in the end leads to feeling shamed and alone ... and grasping to blame someone else.

Regardless of what I did, my kids were still going to throw deck chairs at each other from time to time, and I'd need to turn to God for comfort. But hopefully I won't root around for some stones to throw in my own face. That won't even occur to me when I am living a humbled life.

Otherwise, what am I saying? That my image, my pride, is more important than God? If I worry what others think, that is fear, and it is as far from my Lord as I can get.

Humility is not humiliation. Shame is something that exists in the dark ... like all those dishes my son used to hide under his bed. Humility is knowing we draw our strength from Him and surrendering our will to His, confident we are born from His perfection, trusting that what happens is His will.

Along those lines, how we react to our challenges should be the same way we react to our triumphs. Feeling exalted on the mountaintop is a rush. It is easy when things are going well. We love to win, and in those moments, we use phrases such as *I'm on top of the world*. It feels great.

Conversely, it's not so fun at the bottom, when we feel the eyes of the world on us and our misbehaving children.

And yet, to God, aren't both types of experiences the same? Isn't God with us when we are happy and when we are sad? Why do we move further from God in our triumphs, thinking we owned that moment, that we made it happen? And when things don't go well, we equally focus on ourselves. We reach out to Him in our misery but still try to control the moment through self-shame and humiliation. Both are acts of control that belong to God, not us.

Wouldn't we be better off feeling grateful no matter our situation? Shouldn't we give ourselves to Him always, in good times and bad, and leave the pride and shame out of the equation?

Verse: "Love is patient, love is kind. It does not envy, it does not boast, it is not proud. It does not dishonor others, it is not self-seeking, it is not easily angered, it keeps no record of wrongs. Love does not delight in evil but rejoices with the truth. It always protects, always trusts, always hopes, always perseveres" (1 Cor. 13:4–7).

Further Reading:

> John 13
> Romans 14
> Ephesians 2
> Ephesians 5

Prayer: Lord, guide me toward self-love. I am Your child—how could I be anything but perfect in Your eyes? Help me avoid self-shame and humiliation as well as pride. With Your guidance, I will be humble yet resilient, loving to myself, and always striving to be better. May I judge myself with kindness but remain steadfast in following You. Amen.

CHAPTER ELEVEN

A "Perfect" Time to Pause

We are now a little past the halfway point in this book, whose point is to exemplify that, compared to my family, yours isn't nearly as messed up as you think. And to prove it, let's take a quiz I like to call How Bad Could It Really Be?

Interested in finding out how you rank as a parent? Curious if you might have succeeded in becoming a "perfect parent"? Take the following quiz to see.

1. How we educate our children says a lot about us. How would you finish this statement? Before my child could tell time, I …

> a. Worked daily with my kid discussing the different clock hands and how to interpret them. I even bonged like a grandfather clock on the hour and half hour.
> b. Bought a book about telling time and occasionally read it to my child.
> c. Took advantage of the situation and told the kids it was their bedtime even though it was really four in the afternoon.

2. Patience is a virtue, especially for parents. When your child is telling a long-winded story without that key ingredient (a point), how do you react?

> a. I love anything that comes out of my child's mouth. Every story is to be treasured and appreciated. I write them all down and keep them in a special journal ... every one of them.
> b. I give my child a specific time limit to speak, during which I provide my full attention.
> c. I've learned to sleep with my eyes open.

3. Children fight—it's a fact of parenting. How we choose to respond to intrafamily squabbles is our choice. What do you do when the little ones have declared World War III on each other?

> a. I sit the children down and discuss how hurtful and demoralizing fighting can be, and then I have them shake hands and promise to find *only* the love in each other.
> b. I tell them to knock it off and stay away from each other until they can be civil.
> c. I lock myself in my bedroom and devour a pint of chocolate ice cream.

4. Treasuring the memories is a task that pays huge dividends in the future. Scrapbooks are an excellent way for parents to preserve those cherished activities and events. What have you done?

a. I have completed books for each child from their first baby shower up to their most recent accomplishments. I even have them color coded.

b. I have a decent scrapbook for my first child, a partially filled one for my second kid, and the book I bought for my third child is still in the wrapper.

c. I have only an unidentified noodle collage in the back seat of the car.

RESULTS

In a nationwide test, most parents answered *b* or *c* to the preceding questions. Those who answered *a* are asked to keep that to themselves.

For me, parenting was a lot harder than I thought it would be.

For me, parenting was a lot harder than I thought it would be.

Before I had children, I'd thought that being a dad was all about snuggling, playing games, and sharing my wisdom with little people who looked like me.

Now I know that that's actually what *grandparenting* is.

Parenting is responsibility. It is about trying to raise children who don't run with scissors and don't chew with their mouths open. It's about teaching courtesy and why you shouldn't hit your friend on the head with a lunch box. It's about allowing your children to fail and telling them no for the thousandth time.

Parenting is about hearing yourself sound like your own parents and yet still believing what you're saying is right. It's about being a modern family living a fast-paced lifestyle fraught with pressures, guilt, and the societal expectations to create the perfect childhood.

Parenting is a job.

Perhaps you are questioning me for saying these things because you have well-behaved children. You're thinking, *How can he call it a job? It's a privilege. Every moment is heaven.*

I agree ... except for the part about heaven. It's more like *hectic.*

Despite the cookie-cutter advice from psychologists, pediatricians, and my mother, I have come to the conclusion that parenting is just plain challenging. Period. There are no easy fixes—no miracles—no obedience classes offered for children. It's all about surviving the toils of daycare, childless coworkers, and muddy footprints on the sofa, only to be rewarded for this hard work by seeing your offspring enter the teenage years!

Why do I mention all this? Because, for a long time, I thought I was the only one who struggled with the job of raising children. I figured I was just an idiot; the *one* parent in the world with goofy kids.

Why?

Because other parents *lie.*

Very few people, for whatever reason, will be honest and admit that they have goofy kids too. At the soccer fields, during school field trips, at toddler gym—they don't mention that their kids are flunking math, having trouble making friends, or still not potty trained even though they're five. They keep these things to themselves, going so far as to look cross-eyed when someone admits the truth.

Maybe they're embarrassed or worried that it reflects poorly on them.

What I've learned, however, is that every family struggles in some way with raising children. It's just a part of the job. It's okay. If everything were perfect, we wouldn't have those great character wrinkles.

I have decided, therefore, to move on to chapter 12 with even more stories about my family life so you won't feel quite so alone. I mean, that is, if you don't have a perfect family. You don't, do you? Please tell me you don't!

CHAPTER TWELVE

Bless the Beasts and the Children

I have to laugh when people without children think they can relate to parents because they own a dog.

"Do you have children?"

"Yes, we have a dog."

They say this with complete seriousness as if, at that very moment, their dog is home teething. They'll also say things like:

"We bought a dog to see what parenting is like."

Or:

"If we can raise a dog, we can raise a child."

Or my favorite:

"We're going to space out the ages of our children. When Spot is five, we'll have another child."

To which I always want to reply: "So, how's Spot's diaper rash?"

Where did they get the idea that children are that easy to raise? Don't they remember being kids themselves? Have they never set foot inside a Chuck E. Cheese?

The only thing dogs are going to prepare these people for are when their nieces and nephews come over to visit. Quiet, demure, introverted nephews and nieces, that is.

Most dog owners understand this. After all, a dog is considered a best friend. Children are not best friends. And for good reason. Could you imagine telling your best friend to put on clean underwear? And when's the last time a best friend woke you up from a nap by burping in your face?

Sure, dogs can be messy. They jump on the furniture, lick your face, and they don't like taking a bath ... just like kids. But unlike with children, if you make your dogs spend the night outside by themselves, CPS couldn't care less. Dogs eat the same food day in and day out without complaining. And they don't microwave ice cream cartons (long story).

So, for those still confused, I supply my Top Ten Reasons Why Dogs Are *Much* Easier to Raise Than Children:

> 1. Dogs play-fight with their siblings, and no one gets hurt. Older children give their brothers and sisters Indian burns until someone cries.
>
> 2. Dogs don't complain about other dogs. "It's not fair! Rover's parents bought *him* a new collar. It has studs all over it!"
>
> 3. Dogs don't know the words to the fart song. But even if they did, they wouldn't sing it while Grandma was blowing out her birthday candles.
>
> 4. Dogs get worms. Kids *eat* worms.
>
> 5. Dogs *are* supposed to eat scraps off the floor.

6. Dogs look cute when they're in trouble.

7. Dogs have obedience schools where they learn not to beg, whine, or torture the cat.

8. It takes only a small, five-cent treat to get a dog to do what you ask him ... the first time.

9. Dogs never get tired of being excited to see you. Try to get a teenager to act that way!

10. Two words: invisible fencing.

I hope this helps clarify the issue for those who still think that the dog on the end of your leash is like a child. If not, borrow someone's kids and take them for a walk this week. See what happens when you tell them to heel.

Cats, on the other hand, are definitely more like kids. I am not saying that children are easier to raise than cats, because, as everyone knows, cats are the easiest things in the world to raise ... except for maybe zucchini. But I am suggesting that it's likely that genetic researchers and scientists have it all wrong about humans and apes. I think that it's quite possible that at one time, cats and children were on the identical evolutionary line.

Sure, you could argue that this can't be true because cats walk on four legs, hiss, and eat off the floor ... but then again, you haven't met my children. But I'll take it one step further and offer you ten reasons why cats are like children.

1. Cats hate to take baths, and so do most boys.

2. Cats hack up hair balls and leave them lying around in the middle of the living room floor ten

minutes before guests arrive. Children do this with their toenail clippings.

3. One minute, cats are sitting lovingly in your lap, purring their little brains out, and in the next, they are digging their claws into your flesh ... just like teenagers.

4. Cats toy with their prey. Children toy with their parents.

5. Cats sometimes look at you as if you are the dumbest living thing on the planet. (See #3.)

6. Cats and children both enjoy the finer things in life, like eating bugs, drinking from mud puddles, and sitting in trees.

7. Both cats and children taunt the neighbor dog—as long as there is a fence separating the two.

8. Cats stop playing with the toys you buy them roughly five minutes after you give the toy to them ... sound familiar?

9. Four words: climbing on the counters.

10. Cats lick themselves ... need I say more?

I hope this helps clarify why at times when you are in a rush, you may accidentally call one of your children by the cat's name.

Speaking of cats, over the past thirty years, my family has had three cats. I didn't have cats growing up, but when my bride and I found a kitten only a few days old in the back of a friend's pickup truck, we happily claimed her for our own. We named her Rosemary.

We brought her to our apartment, where she faithfully adopted us as well as the entire apartment community.

A few years later, we moved to our first home, and then five years after that, we moved to our present abode, which butts up to a protected marsh. Rosemary turned ten the same summer night that she disappeared. We suspected foul play. Namely, we assumed either she was taken by a pack of coyotes that planned to raise her like one of their own (which we told the kids) or the coyotes ate her.

Unfortunately, the next cat we adopted from the local shelter didn't fare too well either. We had Louie for less than a summer before he, too, went missing, this time during the day. We kept him in at night thinking we could outwit the band of canines. However, they were obviously casing our place waiting for their chance to take another hostage (the kids didn't buy that one either).

When we brought home kitty number three, Lucy, we knew what we had to do … raise an indoor cat. It was not only better for our feline friend but also easier on the children, who were getting a little upset that their pets kept getting eaten.

Unfortunately, indoor cats create two major issues for a family.

1. Stinky kitty litter boxes.
2. Stinky kitty litter boxes that trigger your gag reflex.

Having had cats that did their business outside, we were unprepared for the watery eyes, raw smells, and our children refusing to come in at night.

"We can't breathe in there!" they shouted from the front lawn.

"You'll get eaten by coyotes if you stay outside," I yelled back. "Haven't you learned anything?"

"You said they were all kidnapped! Are you saying our cats were … were …?"

We knew we had to do something. I suggested wearing full scuba gear around the house, but my wife had a different plan. She returned home from the pet store with a kitty litter box the size of an end table. It had a motorized shovel that circled the interior box, scooping up *ahem*, and dropping it into a concealed, odor-free compartment for later removal. It was the aircraft carrier of kitty litter boxes. I called it Moe. Moe cost $90.

"I wonder," I said as the cat and I watched my wife demonstrate the machine.

"Wonder what?" my wife asked.

"I wonder if it would have been cheaper to just get the cat a colostomy bag."

She wasn't amused. Neither was the cat.

Moe lasted eight months before refusing to budge one more inch. The sand and grit jammed his mechanism. Which was good, because I had strained my lower back fifty-seven times trying to carry Moe outside to wash him out.

Now before you cat fanatics write me with your suggestions to the problem (or yell at me for the colostomy crack), let me say that yes, we love our cat, and yes, we'll do anything to keep her safe. We've significantly upgraded the quality of Lucy's food (which helped a bit); we use cedar chips in the (now smaller) kitty litter box; and *of course*, we have air fresheners plugged into every single outlet in our home.

So, what's the point of this, you ask?

I like outdoor cats better.

REFLECTION

There is nothing in the Bible to concretely suggest that our pets go to heaven and that, one day, we will be reunited with them. I guess we will just have to wait to find out. But I do like this section from Isaiah 11 regarding the effects of living fully in Jesus:

> The wolf will live with the lamb,
>   the leopard will lie down with the goat,
> the calf and the lion and the yearling together;
>   and a little child will lead them.
> The cow will feed with the bear,
>   their young will lie down together,
>   and the lion will eat straw like the ox.
> The infant will play near the cobra's den,
>   and the young child will put its hand into the
>   viper's nest.
> They will neither harm nor destroy
>   on all my holy mountain,
> for the earth will be filled with the knowledge of
>   the LORD
>   as the waters cover the sea. (Isa. 11:6–9)

Did you notice that the child put his hand in the viper's nest? I bet his mom and dad warned him not to do that!

Verse: "The wolf will live with the lamb, the leopard will lie down with the goat, the calf and the lion and the yearling together; and a little child will lead them" (Isa. 11:6).

Further Reading:

> Genesis 9
> Matthew 25
> Philippians 2:4

Prayer: Lord, I understand that all living things are within my sphere of influence. Help me to be dedicated today to protect them all. May I offer careful, kind, and loving stewardship of this earth as praise to You for Your creation. It is not for me to pick or choose. I am here only to love. Guide me, Lord, in this quest. Amen.

CHAPTER THIRTEEN

Raising Cain

Not everyone knows this, but boys are genetically predisposed to do dumb things.

It's true.

Two boys walking down the street, for example, will suddenly (but instinctively) grab each other's arms and spin around and around like a merry-go-round. And just when the two are laughing their heads off, with no warning at all, one will let go of the other, sending the boy careening out of control into a sticker bush.

This is called "fun" in a boy's world.

Even the kid in the sticker bush loves it. At least, after he's done crying.

All males do this. It just looks different at various age levels. Teenagers and grown men prefer more civilized contact games, like basketball and tackle football. Younger boys, on the other hand, prefer to push their friends into doggy doo-doo.

Another reason boys tend to play rough is because they don't have innate social skills.

If they are in the middle of a Monopoly game, and one boy (usually the one losing) doesn't want to play anymore, rarely will he excuse himself from play or politely suggest they put the board aside and occupy their time in some other fashion. Instead, he will make startling machine-gun sounds, scream *"Hit the dirt!"* and fling his body onto the game board. This creates instant pandemonium, and parents come running, only to discover four boys rolling around on the floor trying to jam little plastic green houses up each other's noses.

Behavioral scientists call this "bonding."

Parents call it "time for bed."

When not intentionally hitting one another, boys love to simulate doing so. They pretend they are Batman, secret agents, or kung-fu experts, and they make-believe they are fighting by punching and kicking in slow motion. This is the worst, because invariably, someone extends his punch or kick too far and makes contact, thus hurting someone else who wasn't prepared to take the punch. Boys play that game constantly … in the house, in the backyard, at church, during weddings, at the DMV.

I once made the mistake of taking my son and his friend to the grocery store, where they reenacted famous Indiana Jones scenes … in the frozen foods.

I was, of course, ignoring their behavior until my son yelled, "Ow, Stephen, you kneed my privates!"

It's not easy to recover in public after that, especially when the patients from a convalescent home are there on a field trip.

Strangely, though, boys act shocked when someone gets hurt.

> Child: That couldn't have hurt. I barely touched him!
> Parent: Then how come Sean is in a fetal position sucking his thumb?

While dads can relate to this behavior (of course remembering their share of dogpiles and noogies as kids), moms don't understand it at all.

"Why do they like beating on each other?" my wife once asked me.

"It's how boys express friendship."

"Well, our son's class pictures came back, and he has more scabs and bruises than any other boy in his class."

"Wow!" I exclaimed. "He must be really popular."

She looked at me, displeased. "And so, what happens if your son ends up in the hospital, huh?"

"Well, then," I said, "I guess he'd be a shoo-in for class president."

Funny, she wasn't as excited as I was. I should've given her a noogie for that.

The great military strategist Sun Tzu (c. 544–496 BC) once stated:

> If your enemy is secure at all points, be prepared for him. If he is superior in strength, evade him. If your opponent is of choleric temperament, seek to irritate him. Pretend to be weak, that he may grow arrogant. If he is taking his ease, give him no rest. If his forces are united, separate them.... Attack him where he is unprepared, appear where you are not expected.[2]

Little did I know that Sun Tzu was writing this for my son Alasdair, who, from this point forward, I shall call Sun Menace.

When he was young, Sun Menace thought he was a great samurai. To prove it, he'd take a stick, an empty wrapping-paper tube, or anything else that could leave a mark, and start waving it in front of his body and over his head at a frighteningly fast velocity, pretending he was a Japanese warlord surrounded by Mongols. He'd make high-pitched squeals, cut the air with jabs and slices, and scare the heck out of the cat.

Rarely would there be any warning. Not even Sun Menace knew when it was time to be a shogun. On any normal day, he'd just move through life, listening to his music or scavenging the kitchen for food ... and then it would happen. In his path would be a sword-like object. It could've been a broom, a yard-sign stake, or the antenna from his RC car. It didn't matter what it was, so long as he could swing it in a full range of motion like a windmill.

He couldn't help but pick up the "sword" and engage his invisible enemy.

The problem, of course, was that all too often the rest of us in the family tended to play the part of the Mongols. Not intentionally, of course. We just sometimes accidentally walked into the middle of his duels ... forgetting to cover our faces.

> Son: *Hi-ya!*
> Me: (oof) ... nice, *gasp*, swordsmanship, son. Now, help me find my contact lens.

It was like this since he was three.

Of course, to be fair, Sun Menace wasn't always a samurai. Sometimes he was a Knight of the Round Table, a soldier with a bayonet, or (my favorite) a ninja who haunted the dark … even if it was in my bathroom.

I was told by experts that many boys like to play-fight and that I should learn to grin and bear it. I tried to do so, when I wasn't holding my head back to stop the bleeding.

Once, as I was rubbing the abrasion on my bald spot, I started wondering about parents who have only daughters. What did they do for excitement? What would it be like to walk around your house without having to look over your shoulder? Did it feel strange to *not* have a nervous tick? Did they get a break on their health insurance?

There's never a good time to receive a phone call in your car from your son when the conversation begins with the words "Dad, the police want to know when you are coming home."

Experts say 10 percent of highway rollovers stem from such announcements.

"The policeman left his phone number, and he wants you to call him," my son continued. "Dad? Dad, are you still there?"

"What?" I asked, clearing my spinning mind seconds before hitting a cement truck. "W-why do the police want to talk to me?"

"I don't know," my son replied, as if that was going to satisfy my curiosity. "Maybe because my friends and I were lighting matches at the bus stop this morning?"

To make a long story short, that about covered it. A neighbor who witnessed the boys tossing the flaming matches into the street had visited the school and picked my son and his pyro friends out of the yearbook. To make matters worse, before the boys had been called into the principal's office, they'd also threatened another kid from the same bus stop. They'd told the poor sixth grader to keep quiet and not squeal or they'd beat him up … and *that* was why the police were coming to my house. *Ugh.*

But that wasn't why I was upset. I knew that any threat my son made was only a figure of speech. And it was appropriate that he was called to the carpet for what he said. What I didn't appreciate, however, was the sequence of events that transpired once the police officer knocked on our door.

The officer walked casually into our living room where my son sat sheepishly on the couch. As the officer put his hands on his hips, I turned to my son and said sternly, "I want you to answer this officer's questions honestly and then take to heart everything he has to say. Do you understand me?"

For the next five minutes, the officer, in the most neutral tone I can imagine, explained to my teenage boy not only the dangers of playing with matches but also the seriousness of making threats. He told my son that the other boy was "truly scared" and that the police take every threat seriously. He said my son wouldn't get off so easily the next time. Then, the officer left.

See why I was shocked? Like any dad worth his salt, when the officer had crossed my threshold, I'd been hoping for one thing and one thing only.

I wanted the cop to take out his handcuffs and pretend he was taking my son to jail.

Those couple of moments of sheer panic would've done more to teach my son a lesson than anything I could've ever devised.

But no such luck. Officer Friendly didn't lose his composure once. Where were the harsh words? The threats? The flying spittle?

Don't get me wrong: I didn't want the officer to hit my son with his nightstick. But making my teenager cry would have been helpful. Sure, I grounded my son and piled on the chores. But weeding the yard doesn't make a kid wet his pants like a good pat-down would've.

My wife thought the cop's lecture was appropriate.

Yeah, well, as a dad and a taxpayer, I was outraged!

Next time, I am hiring an actor.

My wife, Allison, and I once embarked on a daring expedition. Boldly but with great trepidation, we ventured into the vast unknown wilderness known as our youngest son's bedroom.

Frankly, we deserve to have a statue carved in our honor.

To be honest, we hadn't seen his bedroom for quite some time. Or at least, we hadn't seen his floor. Talk about a disaster. You couldn't fully open his bedroom door because of the mess. How he crossed to his bed without killing himself is one of those great puzzles of modern-day life ... a mystery my wife and I were determined to solve. So, when our son was away for the day, we broke camp and set forth on a mission rivaling that of Lewis and Clark.

Captain's log: December 30—9:08 a.m.
After a breakfast of roots and berries, Allison and I donned thick-soled shoes and hacked our way through the pile of clothes,

cardboard, comic books, and silly string blocking the entrance to our son's bedroom. Strange plant life near the doorway. Could be moss. Could be toast. I grab whatever it is and press it into our botanical scrapbook.

Captain's log: December 30—9:12 a.m.
I suck in my gut and squeeze through the small, allowable space between the door and doorjamb, thus entering the bedroom for the first time since I can remember. It's a strange, unfamiliar land full of mystery and an odor that makes my eyes burn. Allison, tied to me by rope, is close on my heels. We are in awe of our discovery as we go where no other human has gone before.

Captain's log: December 30—9:25 a.m.
Allison finds her long-lost salad tongs … or, at least, half of them. Next, we take samples of clothing on the floor to determine whether they are clean or dirty. That task proves more difficult than anticipated. When finished, in the dirty pile are two items—a sock and my sweater. The clean pile nearly reaches to the ceiling. I take pictures of our findings and then trip over a tackle box.

Captain's log: December 30—9:40 a.m.
More bad luck hits the expedition. From the bunk bed, a fast-moving avalanche of papers and candy wrappers buries Allison. I dig her out with a broken tennis racket. Further investigation reveals it's *my* tennis racket.

Captain's log: December 30—9:53 a.m.
We enter our son's closet. I drop pieces of Halloween candy I find under my son's bed behind us so we can find our way back out. Scaling a three-foot heap of old toys, furniture, and trash, we slide down the back side and get wedged helplessly into the corner. We survive on Halloween candy until our son returns home and rescues us.

Watch your local retailer for T-shirts of the Swarner Expedition.

When my nephew Nolan was three, he had his tonsils and adenoids removed. The surgery went smoothly, but by that evening, my nephew had developed a small fever and become Mr. Cranky Pants. He spent the next three days on the family room couch transitioning from whining to crying and back to whining.

My sister played nursemaid during those days, taking time off work to watch over her little guy. This job included bringing my nephew refreshments and performing hourly shows, such as singing nursery rhymes, turning the Snoopy Sno-cone maker, and reading *Green Eggs and Ham* over and over and over …

Sometime around the ninety-eighth hour, just as my sister was ready to collapse (or steal one of her son's Vicodin pills), my nephew showed strong signs of recovery. In other words, he stuck a bead up his nose.

The retired paramedic who lived next door, however, didn't really care why my nephew had done this (nor did he ask why the Vicodin bottle was in my sister's hand). Instead, he said in paramedic-speak, "I don't feel good about attempting to fish that impacted bead out of your son's nostril."

This was good news to my nephew, who also didn't want the big, burly medic to go after the bead. Instead, my nephew insisted that his mother remove the bead.

This, of course, was the fifteenth demand my sister had received that day from her family … a list that didn't get any shorter when she tried calling her husband on the golf course but failed to make a connection with him because his cell phone "happened" to go on the blink that very day.

Unfortunately, there wasn't time to curse the broken cell phone, because my sister now needed to load my nephew with the bead up his nose—together with her other son, six-year-old Drew (laughing at his brother with the bead up his nose)—into her car and drive them all to the emergency room.

Which (surprise, surprise) was packed with other hysterical parents facing a myriad of similar crises with their children.

As they waited to see a physician, my nephews fought over the Richard Scarry books in the waiting room. Finally, they were escorted into an examination room, where an admitting nurse weighed and measured the three-year-old, while the six-year-old tried building a log cabin out of tongue depressors.

This, however, is where our story takes a sudden turn. As my sister explained to the nurse how the whole bead-up-the-nose situation related to the tonsil and adenoid surgery, my three-year-old nephew suddenly held up the snotty bead and exclaimed, "Look, Mommy, it popped out!" … thus inciting a victory dance on a gurney by the six-year-old.

Not that the receptionist in charge of admitting at the emergency room took the children's "joy" into consideration when she told my sister, "Yes, in fact, you do have to pay for the emergency room visit, even though you didn't see a doctor."

And then it was home for everyone.

Finally, if you are like I was when my kids were young, you might have sent a boy to camp and, despite your many messages, found that he wouldn't reply to you with a text or email until you wrote your messages IN ALL CAPS.

I don't see what is so difficult about sending a note home. It's not like I asked my children to clean their rooms or stop walking into the house with muddy shoes.

So, just in case you missed out on a decent letter from your son this summer too, I give you the following to scan and email to yourself. I hope it helps.

> Dear (insert your name or title),
> Hello from Camp Winnemucka. I am having a great time. I miss you very much. Give the dog a kiss on the lips for me.
> I've been busy every day, swimming, hiking, doing crafts, and making new friends. There

are many interesting people in my cabin. I met a kid who knows 107 fart jokes. He's a genius. I've memorized 67 so far. There's another kid in my group who can turn his tongue upside down. I wish I could do that. I tried but drooled on myself.

The mosquitoes are really big here. My counselor said one of the six-year-olds got carried off by a mosquito the first day, but I think he was joking. I'm not, however, taking any chances. I have 32 rocks stuffed in my pockets to weigh me down. It's hard to sleep, though.

My friends and I have a contest going to see who can smell the worst by Sunday. The counselor said we were making his eyes water, so he made us shower yesterday. But don't worry, I should still win. I didn't use soap.

During craft classes, I've made three God's eyes, two hand-dipped candles, and seven lanyards. I traded them for candy with a little kid.

The food is okay. I got a stomachache the first night after dinner, but I think I was just homesick.

By the way, guess what *SOS* stands for? My counselor told me. I'd probably better not write down the answer—just in case the government reads this. I'll tell you when I get home.

Well, got to go. After lunch, all of us are going to see who can scream the loudest.

Thanks for sending me to camp. You're the best, and I miss you a lot!!

(Insert child's name)
XXX OOO

REFLECTION

Jesus was divine, but He was also human, and I can't help but wonder what trouble He might have gotten into as a young boy. Was He always "perfectly" behaved?

We do get a glimpse of His life as a twelve-year-old in the story of the temple:

> When Joseph and Mary had done everything required by the Law of the Lord, they returned to Galilee to their own town of Nazareth. And the child grew and became strong; he was filled with wisdom, and the grace of God was on him.
>
> Every year Jesus' parents went to Jerusalem for the Festival of the Passover. When he was twelve years old, they went up to the festival, according to the custom. After the festival was over, while his parents were returning home, the boy Jesus stayed behind in Jerusalem, but they were unaware of it. Thinking he was in their company, they traveled on for a day. Then they began looking for him among their relatives and friends. When they did not find him, they went back to Jerusalem to look

for him. After three days they found him in the temple courts, sitting among the teachers, listening to them and asking them questions. Everyone who heard him was amazed at his understanding and his answers. When his parents saw him, they were astonished. His mother said to him, "Son, why have you treated us like this? Your father and I have been anxiously searching for you."

"Why were you searching for me?" he asked. "Didn't you know I had to be in my Father's house?" But they did not understand what he was saying to them.

Then he went down to Nazareth with them and was obedient to them. But his mother treasured all these things in her heart. And Jesus grew in wisdom and stature, and in favor with God and man. (Luke 2:39–52)

Can you imagine your child missing for three days? I think I'd have more to say than "Your father and I have been anxiously searching for you."

How about Jesus' reply? "Didn't you know I had to be in my Father's house?"

Anyone with a teenager likely understands the anger that might arise from such an answer. I know it's not right to feel that here. Jesus is divine—certainly, we can't expect Him to go into time-out. Still, when I hear His reply, I feel my gut tighten. It sounds like the sarcasm only a teenager can do so well.

I can see Mary's point. Why? Because behind anger with our children is usually something deeper. In this case, probably embarrassment.

Can you imagine getting to the town at nightfall and looking around and your son isn't there? What are the other parents thinking? Mary and Joseph must have felt their judgment.

Today, you are on the news if your child just rides his bike on the neighbor's front lawn. Not your child. *You.*

> Announcer: This just in to the newsroom—Ken Swarner failed to teach his son to stay on the sidewalk, and now the Smiths next door have a birdbath in pieces ... as is Mrs. Smith.
> (Then the news anchor looks into the camera.) Mr. Swarner will likely feel the sting of this humiliation for years. In other news, Swarner's son Jack survived the accident and dreams of the day the front tire on his bike no longer wobbles.

I'm not positive, but surely Mary and Joseph looked around at their caravan that night, dumbfounded. Maybe they offered up excuses. Maybe they blamed each other. Definitely they went berserk and started running back toward Jerusalem.

I understand this moment. I bet many parents who have left a child somewhere by accident do too. When this happens, we feel great shame. And no amount of anger can fix that feeling.

This story also points out the faith and obedience of Mary and Joseph, and the role they played in Jesus' upbringing. We see that Jesus grew strong, happy, and wise.

We can do that for our children as well, by faithfully taking them to church, enrolling them in religious schools or church classes, praying before meals and/or at bedtime, and simply demonstrating faith in our own lives.

How did I do this? Whenever I could, I explained to my children the process I went through to make a decision and how that process was influenced by my understanding of God. I kept Jesus in my words day to day with my kids. I always suggested prayer to them when they were confronted with challenges. I tried not to jam Christianity down their throats. I tried to show the kids how, when I missed the mark, I prayed for forgiveness and solutions. I lived God out loud. If they saw me do it, I knew they just might follow suit.

Verse: "'The virgin will conceive and give birth to a son, and they will call him Immanuel' (which means 'God with us')" (Matt. 1:23).

Further Reading:

> Matthew 2
> Luke 2

Prayer: Lord, help my children know You, not in just what I say, but in my actions as well. I know that even now they are always watching me, especially when it is difficult to do what is right. Guide me to align my words with my deeds—to live out my faith so that they continue to develop theirs. Let me be their spiritual guide by demonstrating Your true way. Amen.

CHAPTER FOURTEEN

Words of Wisdom

My parents gave me plenty of advice on parenting over the years. Talk about nerve!

Especially considering the number of times they tried to kill me when I was a child.

Not intentionally—or *so they say*, and nothing I could prove in a court of law—but the facts speak for themselves.

Take, for example, the seemingly innocent custom of hiding Easter eggs around the house. After "the Easter Bunny" took our colorful masterpieces from the refrigerator and placed them in a variety of room-temperature locations, my folks never once stepped in to control the situation. They didn't even leave a pamphlet for the bunny on proper food-handling techniques.

The eggs stayed under the couches and chairs all night.

Apparently, fifty years ago, grown men and women thought items purchased in the refrigerator section of the grocery store were simply there because shelf space in dry goods was not to be had.

I know my parents must have thought this, because never once did I come padding from my bedroom on Easter morning only to hear them exclaim, "Happy Easter, Kenny! Go find your Easter eggs. And we sure hope you don't get stomach cramps later on."

Where was the alarm? The warning labels? The public health department?

Maybe they weren't trying to snuff me out, but I could probably build a case on negligence.

The list of such instances is long, like the number of times I was left unattended in supermarket parking lots with a mean older brother. Or the hundreds of bike rides I was allowed to take without a helmet. Or the full-sized bars of Ivory soap I ingested due to a smart mouth I *inherited* from my father. And what about the number of times my mother told me to "go play in traffic"? She claims it was only an expression, but I wish I had that on videotape now.

These were also the same folks who, by the way, loaded up the children in the station wagon and drove seventy-five miles per hour down the freeway and never saying a word while us kids played: "Red rover, red rover, send Kenny flying over the seats right over!"

What about seat belts? Who was in charge back then? Where was Uncle Sam?

Why is it that today, parents can't move an inch without a thousand talk shows, CPS, and the PTA having something to say about it, but in the early '70s, my parents could drive a pickup truck with me rolling around in the open bed to the applause and cheers of other parents in the neighborhood as we passed?

For the record, however, I'm not the only one with a potential legal case. Seat belts might have also come in handy when my brother-in-law Dutch was six years old. As family legend has it, his mom hit a tight corner at low speed, and Dutch, who had a well-publicized habit of fiddling with the door handles, fell out of the car.

Incidentally, as he climbed back into his seat, my mother-in-law (who never served jail time, I might add) told him to stop crying or she'd give him something to cry about.

Typical. I could write volumes on parents then and now.

I always crack up when my mom compares her parenting situations to mine, saying something like "Well, I don't ever remember having this much trouble when I was a parent."

That's not surprising. After all, in 1976, gossiping on the phone while watching a soap opera, drinking a Tab, smoking a cigarette, and telling us kids to go play in traffic were considered effective parenting.

My mom didn't mince words back then either. "Gloria, I need to put the phone down a minute, spank my kids, and grab another Tab. I'll be right back."

She wielded a mean wooden spoon. And there was no distinction between spankings and time-out during my youth. Everyone knew back then that *time-out* meant icing down your buttocks.

In those days, moms didn't worry about raising their voices or beating their kids in public. At least, my mom never had any problems calling attention to herself. Occasionally, you'd find her hauling me out of a public place with my arm over my head ... my feet bobbing off the ground like an astronaut walking on the moon.

During those moments, my mom transformed into a mutterer. All the way out the store she'd talk to herself: "I don't know why I had to have kids who can't listen to a word I say. I bet their father is having a nice, quiet day."

If her other hand were free at the time, she'd also punctuate each word with a slap to my butt. "And (*slap*) I'll (*slap*) give (*slap*) you (*slap*) something (*slap*) to (*slap*) cry (*slap*) about (*slap*) (*slap*)!"

Unfortunately, certain defenses never worked for me, such as slumping to the ground like dead weight, also known as the wet noodle. My mom would just keep on going, dragging me across the parking lot.

Now, you'd think that that might inspire someone to intervene on my behalf. But instead, other parents would just yell as I skidded by: "Rotten kid! You're liable to throw out your mother's back, bless her soul!"

The thing is, moms in those days had more solidarity than the Teamsters. No one gave my mom a dirty look or threatened to call Child Protective Services. In the grocery stores, other moms would clear an entire grocery aisle to make room so my mom could get a good range of motion.

And in the checkout line, they'd give her cuts. "Please, dear, you obviously have your hands full with that little monster. Take my place in line."

And if that wasn't enough: "By the way, would you like me to hold your son's arm over his head while you write your check?"

Neighborhood moms, of course, were the worst. They'd do anything to help out. "Joan, you look like you're getting tired. Why don't I spank Kenny while you pour yourself another Tab?"

So where did moms learn all this stuff? My guess is it was at those PTA meetings.

"Okay, ladies, let's start the meeting. After the treasurer's report, Bev is going to share her top five tips for wiping the smile off a smartmouth, and then we'll all enjoy some delicious Bundt cake."

I'm certainly not saying we should return to those days ... but I wish my kids realized how good they had it!

My mom is not the only example of changing times, however. There was the time we were at my in-laws' when my mother-in-law lowered the boom.

"Where's Jim?" my wife asked, looking around the kitchen for her dad.

"He's changing Mitch's diaper," she announced.

My wife's face froze in shock. "Excuse me?"

I had to admit that that *was* surprising news. I had started dating my wife in high school. Back then, I thought of Jim as a cross between a prison warden and Ward Cleaver.

"That can't be," my wife retorted.

Her mother smiled. "It's true."

My wife shook her head in disbelief. "But-but this is not the same man I grew up with," she stammered. "That man violated child labor laws. He worked long hours. He waited to be served. He growled. He …"

"… scared the living daylights out of me," I added.

"Exactly!" she exclaimed. "And now, h-he's changing my nephew's diaper?"

My mother-in-law smiled. "Jim's quite comfortable with it. He said changing a poopie diaper is like changing a tire."

"Wait a minute," I interrupted. "Wait one darn minute. He used the word *poopie*?"

Just then, we heard him leading a parade of giggling, rambunctious grandchildren into the living room.

My wife peered around the corner. She motioned us over to look. "And what about this?" she said, pointing. "Who would have thought that the same man who woke me up at 7:00 a.m. on

Saturdays to mow the lawn, hid my shoes when I left them lying around the house, or missed my school events because he had to work would at this very moment be playing This Little Piggy Went Wee Wee Wee All the Way Home?"

I nodded. "And on his own toes, no less!"

She turned and faced me. "I don't know what to do."

"I do," I retorted. "I'm keeping my shoes on, thank you very much."

We sat staring at him rolling on the floor with the grandkids.

"Nice knee drop, son," I shouted. "Now, give Papa a minute to catch his breath."

My wife gestured. "See what I mean? He lets the kids tear him to shreds. If I so much as looked sideways at him growing up, I was on restriction."

Finally, Jim stood up and announced, "Last one to the cookie jar is the rotten egg."

We jumped out of the way to avoid getting run over.

As Jim passed, my wife grabbed his arm. "You changed Mitch's diaper?" she asked him, as if needing to hear it from his mouth.

A goofy smile spread across his face. Then, as if understanding her point, his face softened and he said, "Look, I worked hard when you were young. I felt I had responsibilities. I missed out on having fun with you kids. I'm not going to make the same mistake now." He then hurried over to the counter, shouting, "I'm the rotten egg! I'm the rotten egg!"

My wife didn't say a word. The tear in her eye said it all.

I can't leave this chapter without addressing the issue of grand-parent names.

Take my nephews, for example. Through a variety of situations, they have ended up with four grandmas. As they opened up Christmas gifts one year and said their thank-yous, an interesting detail came to light. There were thank-yous for Grandma, Grandma, Gammie, and Tee-Tee.

Tee-Tee?

I understand that other cultures call their grandparents by other names than we do. I also know that some of those traditions have carried forth throughout the Western Hemisphere, even to Northern European descendants like my family. But I wasn't aware my nephews were calling someone Tee-Tee.

The boys could have their own Pokémon game.

"Hey, Sammy, I'll trade you a Peekachoo for a Gammie and Tee-Tee."

"Tee-Tee?"

Exactly how does a person acquire such a name?

Better question: How's that going to work one day when my nephew Drew is an adult and loses his grandma at the mall?

> Drew (walking up to the sales counter at Target):
> Excuse me, ma'am, but have you seen my Tee-Tee?
> Saleswoman: No, and if you show me, I'm calling
> the cops.

Come to find out, Tee-Tee is short for *Grandma Teresa* ... hence the *T.* I suppose that makes sense. I'm just glad her name wasn't Penelope.

The other day, I got to wondering what other grandmas are called. My kids have always addressed my wife's mother and my mom as simply Grandma. But I looked on the internet and discovered that Tee-Tee wasn't that odd when compared to what else exists out there. One site had people write in and reveal what their grandchildren called them. On the list were Mia, Honey, Granny, Grandmother, Gammer, Nana, Ma, Nanny, Me-ma, Bugger (I'd be afraid to ask), Bubbie, and my favorite, Booger.

Grandpas were in the same boat. There were all the regular names, plus Poppy, Baba, Pa, Pawsy, Da-daddy, Gramps, Pee-Pa, and even a Dave.

Then it struck me. What happens now that I'm a grandpa? What are my grandkids going to call me?

"Goofy," my wife said.

I could end up being a Poopie, I suppose. Or maybe Ken—or worse, Kee-Kee.

How's that going to sound in public?

"Mom, when are Gammie and Kee-Kee coming to pick me up?"

Or "I'd like you to meet my Kee-Kee."

Or "Kee-Kee, party of five? Your table is ready."

I could have an Oscar winner for a granddaughter someday. She would stand on the podium in front of millions of people to thank her Kee-Kee for all his support, and everyone would wonder, *Why is she thanking her cat?*

I don't know how it happened, but my mother turned seventy-five, and ever since, she's been sharing death stories practically every time I see her.

"Ken, I thought you'd like to know that my neighbor Mrs. Benjamin passed away."

It's like she's all of a sudden a walking obituary notice. I can't visit her without hearing the rundown on who was diagnosed with a terminal disease or horrible affliction—or just outright died.

"Ken, remember your third-grade teacher, Mrs. Peterson? Hold my hand."

Frankly, it bums me out. I'm just coming over for dinner or to drop off the kids, and I'm hit with the news of poor David Reynolds, who can no longer tend the rose garden he so dearly loved.

The announcements always start off the same way. My mom can be discussing the weather or a new book she's reading, when suddenly, out of the clear blue, she dramatically pauses with this serious look on her face as if she's about to tell me *she's* got only six weeks to live. It catches me off guard: "Mom, what's wrong? Is there something you're afraid to tell me? Are you sick?"

"Heavens no, Ken. Why? Do I look sick? Speaking of—did I tell you that your best friend in kindergarten, Scott Hutchinson, had a heart attack last week? Wasn't he younger than you?"

My mother also shares death stories about people she's never met.

"I agree it's sad, Mom—but you didn't even know your dermatologist's massage therapist."

And she always acts as if it were her best friend who passed.

"Mom, you haven't even seen her for fifteen years."

"I know, but I feel a piece of me went with poor Jo-Anne."

"It was Joan."

"Whatever."

My mother-in-law is the same way. She is known in certain circles as the Paul Revere of death notices. If you see her coming, it's time to break out a tissue.

Of course, I wonder how it is that they always have a new death story to tell. I never hear the same story twice from their mouths. Is there an underground Death and Disease Network? Are they streaming twenty-four hours on demand somewhere?

"This just in: Rufus Jackson's prostate gained a pound this week."

Even when it's a slow news week and no one is on their deathbed, my mother manages to have some dire story to share.

"Did I tell you about John Phillips?" she asked me.

"Is he dying too, Mom?"

"Oh, good gracious no!" she exclaimed. "But I heard he has a real bad foot fungus."

"You heard?"

"His wife, Martha, apparently moved in with her sister. She says she won't come home until John's feet stop stinking."

I'm not sure how much longer I can take all this.

I don't know if it's that most of the people my mother knows are getting terminal illnesses and dying or that as she gets closer to the end of her own life, death has started preoccupying her thoughts.

Either way, the woman needs a hobby!

REFLECTION

Grandparenting is an awesome responsibility. Free of the need to rear the child, most grandparents can devote their ministry to mentoring and cheerleading. It's a great gig, and not just because you don't have to do the midnight feedings and science-fair projects.

Research says that a healthy transition to retirement includes going from parent-worker to mentor. I used the term *ministry* purposely. Grandparents typically have the time and patience not only to devote their attention to their grandchildren but also to have discussions about God—to mentor them in the Christian faith.

It's in those quiet moments, lying on your backs and pointing out the shapes in the clouds, when children have questions. Grandparents can be there to hear them. G-ma and G-pa are in a great position to answer those inquiries.

With that said, I realize that grandparents don't always have the permission of their adult children to discuss religion with their grandkids. Give it time and prayer. I recently became a grandfather for the first time, and my adult son doesn't have any plans to raise his kids in a Christian home. Obviously, that causes pain for his mother and me. But when the discussion of baptism came up, we simply asked if we could have our grandson baptized. We kept it simple and without any judgment. He agreed. We are hopeful for the future.

Grandparents can be the one thing in a child's life that comes without strings attached. We can love the little ones without condition. Every child deserves that—to have someone in their lives who doesn't pass judgment, no matter what decisions they make. Believe me, we all feel judged by friends, strangers, and even our parents. What a blessing to know someone (besides God) who loves us unconditionally.

> **Grandparents can be the one thing in a child's life that comes without strings attached. We can love the little ones without condition. Every child deserves that.**

We also never stop being grandchildren, do we? Though I'm not that little kid in the school play or batting ninth on the Little League team anymore, I still enjoy the praise my grandparents provided, even though all four of my grandparents have now passed.

I've learned that our grandparents' role does not end just because we've moved out of our childhood homes. Grandparents are still cheerleaders who get excited about everything their grandchildren accomplish ... even when those grandchildren are adults.

While they aren't still there singing my praises in person, I have the memories of their adoration. My grandparents bragged about me to everyone they met, even though I've lived a modest life. They were impressed with my career, family, and even when I bought a new car. They rarely got tired of talking about me. Heck, they would have grabbed up pom-poms and cheered at my corporate awards ceremony if they weren't concerned about breaking their hips.

A grandparent even refutes all those claims brought by Mom or Dad that we are irresponsible with our money or that we aren't raising our children correctly. You can't beat it when Grandma or Grandpa chimes in to say we are doing just fine.

In our adult worlds of responsibility and pressures, when our own children ask us to duck when driving by their friends on the street, it's nice to know there's someone out there who thinks we are still the best thing since sliced bread (and they would know).

Verse: "A good person leaves an inheritance for their children's children" (Prov. 13:22).

Further Reading:

Psalm 92
Proverbs 16

Prayer: Lord, I am so blessed by You to have not only children but grandchildren as well. I pray for the wisdom and guidance to fulfill my duties as a Christian guide. Remind me daily, Lord, of my awesome role as mentor. Help me love them unconditionally—to be their safe harbor—to lead by example and leave judgment to You. Allow me to provide that place where they can be themselves, reveling in the good grace of their divine birthright. Amen.

CHAPTER FIFTEEN

The Reason for the Season

The first year my wife and I were married, we had one of those serious holiday conversations young couples often have.

"My mom wants us to come to her house for Thanksgiving dinner, and your mom wants us to come to her house," my wife announced. "There's only one solution."

I nodded. "Move."

"No, we eat two dinners," she said. "I'll get my mom to serve dinner at four, then we'll rush over to your mom's and eat at seven."

The idea made sense. Neither family would feel left out on Thanksgiving, and my wife and I wouldn't have to choose.

"We'll just have to pace ourselves," I said. "And wear stretchy pants."

The moms agreed.

We showed up at my in-laws' for the first meal Thanksgiving afternoon. The spread smelled and looked wonderful. But just before taking our seats, I reminded my wife of the plan.

"Now, remember, don't eat too much. We have another one of these in a few hours, and we don't want to disappoint my mom because all we have room for left in our stomachs is an antacid."

She nodded, and then we both dived in with reckless abandon. To say we licked our plates clean would be telling secrets. We couldn't help ourselves—we always overeat on Thanksgiving. Of course, in years past, we also had plenty of time afterward to moan on the couch with the rest of the adults.

Not that year. Right after my second slice of pie, my wife announced it was time to go.

I stared at her in shock. "Now?"

"We promised to be at your mom's by six thirty," she replied, chewing on a couple of Alka-Seltzers. "Get off the floor and let's go."

I had to moan all by myself on the drive across town. My wife would have joined me, but she was too busy praying for "one good belch."

We arrived at my mom's house like two people ready to face the firing squad. We knew there was no way we could avoid eating this second dinner, but we also knew how traumatic it might be for the children in the family if Uncle Ken and Auntie Allison exploded during the meal.

My mom was sympathetic. "I hope you didn't eat too much over at Allison's folks' house. I made all your favorites, Ken."

I smiled weakly and lied. "I'm starving."

I can still remember quite vividly how I felt as I shoveled food in my mouth while glancing around the table, hoping someone knew CPR.

I leaned into my wife and asked, "Are you okay?"

She winced. "I can't feel my toes."

Then, during dessert, there was a loud popping noise. At first, I thought my dad had opened another bottle of champagne, but it turned out to be my pants' button bursting.

On the drive home, I told my wife that if I should die in my sleep that night, I'd like my tombstone to read: "He had but one dinner to give."

She pulled her head in from the window and replied, "Try, 'He died with gravy on his chin.'"

For the first twenty years of our marriage, my wife and I had an ironclad set of rituals and traditions during the holidays so our parents got their "fair share" of us. Because our families both lived in town, we alternated various holidays with them. One Easter, for example, we had dinner with my side of the family. So the next year, we went to my wife's parents' house. Pretty simple!

Christmas was a little more complicated, but it worked. The years we visited my parents on Christmas Eve, we'd see my wife's family for Christmas dinner. Then, the next Christmas, we'd switch the order.

I admit the holidays, under that plan, became monotonous. But at least we always knew where we'd be, and both sets of parents felt like they received their equal share.

But then, after more than forty years of marriage, my parents divorced. That really threw the holiday schedule for a loop. Because my parents now live apart, we have an extra household to work into the rotation.

When this first came to light, my mother-in-law asked how it would work. My wife told her that our holiday schedule would need amending and so she should not expect to see us as much on the holidays as she had in the past.

In these situations, it's always helpful to have family who understand the situation and can accept that the old way of doing things is just no longer possible. At least, that's what I would imagine to be true.

"*I* didn't get divorced!" my mother-in-law told my wife. "So why do I have to suffer?"

Of course, this upset my wife. So she stewed for hours trying to rework arrangements and come up with a plan that would make everyone happy. After several drafts, she finally decided that we'd spend Christmas Eve with my dad and get up at the crack of dawn on Christmas morning to open gifts. Then we'd hurry across town to visit my mom to have Christmas lunch and do presents. Finally, we'd jump in the car and race to my wife's parents for Christmas dinner and more presents.

This must be how the tradition of spiking the eggnog started.

When she was finished laying out her ideas, my wife asked for my opinion.

"I thought Christmas was a day for peace on earth?" I replied. "Your schedule sounds like I'd better wake up Christmas morning and stretch."

She frowned. "Do you have a better plan, Ken?"

I shrugged. "You're sure that leaving town isn't an option?"

She said it was important for the children to spend time with their grandparents during the holidays—even if they got cramps running from one house to the next.

After that first year, I told my wife we were joining the Witness Protection Program.

She agreed.

Need another reason to spike the eggnog? Christmas Eve. Take one of mine from those days, for example.

7:00 a.m.: The children wake up my wife and me begging to open their gifts a day early. To which I usually reply, "What gifts?"

8:20 a.m.: I walk groggily downstairs to find the kids shaking their presents. I tell them that Santa hasn't left the North Pole, so there's still time to add them to the Naughty List.

8:21 a.m.: The children explain that they're too old to worry about the Naughty List, and could they please open their gifts now!

8:22 a.m.: I find my wife hiding under our bed covers. I inform her that I am not doing this alone ... so I join her under the bed covers.

8:24 a.m.: The kids find our hiding place.

9:04 a.m., 9:19 a.m., 9:55 a.m., and 10:15 a.m.: My son asks if we can open gifts now.

9:05 a.m., 9:20 a.m., 9:56 a.m., and 10:16 a.m.: I answer, "No," "I said no," "No means *no!*" and "Do you really want to see Daddy cry on Christmas Eve?" respectively.

11:00 a.m.: The Christmas tree looks like it is leaning. There's an eerie calm in the house.

11:05 a.m.: My son runs through the kitchen with *my* Christmas stocking on his head, while my daughter follows, shouting, "Can we open presents now?"

11:49 a.m.: I explain to my wife that I know it's the season of joy, but in all fairness, she can't spend the day listening to Christmas carols and reading her book ... in the back seat of the car.

12:41 p.m.: My daughter says that if we were in Japan, it wouldn't be too early to open our presents ... "Hint, hint."

1:33 p.m.: My son ties his little brother to a chair with curling ribbon.

1:54 p.m.: I pretend to call the Salvation Army and loudly ask, "Are you still accepting gifts this close to Christmas? Because I have a tree full you can have."

1:56 p.m.: I overhear my son tell his sister, "You know, it just doesn't feel like Christmas until Dad calls the Salvation Army."

3:44 p.m.: My daughter says she'll be my best friend if we can open presents now.

3:45 p.m.: My son says he'll give me five bucks if we can open presents now.

3:46 p.m.: My daughter says she'll give me twenty bucks if we can open presents now.

3:47 p.m.: My son says he'll tell me where Mom is hiding if we can open presents now.

3:48 p.m.: I realize that if we were in Japan, it *also* wouldn't be too early to drink a hot toddy.

4:23 p.m.: The Christmas tree is leaning even more.

5:15 p.m.: Our local news channel reports that a mom found a "unique solution" for dealing with her overexcited children on Christmas Eve. She gives them NyQuil.

5:16 p.m.: I discover we are out of NyQuil.

7:30 p.m.: I find the children sitting at the top of the stairs holding a brown cardboard sign that reads: "Will do chores to open gifts right now."

7:31 p.m.: I smile warmly to the children and invite them down to the living room, after finding their mother's hiding place. We gather next to the Christmas tree, and I deliver my annual Christmas Eve reading, which begins with the words "'Twas the night before Christmas when all through the house, not a creature was stirring … because they were all taking Dad to the hospital."

Ahhhh … don't you love tradition?

Of course, I really had to hand it to my children one particular Christmas.

Believe it or not, and please don't feel jealous, but that year my little cherubs made it all the way to January 9 before they stopped playing with the Christmas toys they just had to have.

Pinch me—I must have been dreaming.

Quite frankly, I thought such things happened only in storybooks or on Target commercials. Especially considering what happened that one year after I'd endured ten hours in a line at Walmart to buy *the* toy of the Christmas season—mechanical yipping dogs that my kids stopped playing with on December 29.

The year before it had been Pokémon. On December 30, my son threw the cards on his bedroom floor, sighed, and professed he was bored.

They've been there ever since.

That's why I planned a big celebration to honor my children's commitment. All offspring of mine who spent from late September to December 24 pleading for particular toys, and then took fifteen whole days out of their busy schedules to actually *play* with those things, deserved a big thank-you in my book.

And I told them this when they finally announced they were bored.

"Kids, you have made your daddy proud."

My son eyed me suspiciously. "Why?"

"Because, for starters, I just found your new Karate Chop Man under the deck outside," I answered, smiling giddily from cheek to cheek.

"That's a good thing?"

"It *is* when it wasn't there yesterday," I replied. "Did you know that Christmas Day was over two weeks ago?"

"Huh?"

"Oh sure, I had my doubts in the beginning, but you certainly proved me wrong. Just think, back in September, as the leaves began to fall from our trees, who would have thought that when you told me how badly you wanted a Karate Chop Man action figure for Christmas that it would have brought you such extended joy?

"Even throughout October and November, when I found Karate Chop Man ads stuffed inside my shoes, taped to the cutting board, crinkling inside my pillow, and staring at me in the shower, I thought it was simply another passing phase. I guess, in retrospect, I should have known better. After all, that Karate Chop Man mask you made was darn innovative and a real testament to your desire to have the action figure. Okay, maybe I wish you hadn't slipped the mask on me when I was sleeping, especially since I thought something was attacking my face, and my screams woke up your mother. But heck, how can I be mad about that now?

"I still don't like the Karate Chop Man impressions you did to the back of my head in the car all the way to Grandma's house on Thanksgiving Day, but let's not split hairs. The point is, you wanted the Karate Chop Man, and by darn, that's what you got. And now, as the Karate Chop Man lies under the deck in a puddle, I will pass his final resting place every day, put my hand over my heart, and hope that the fifteen days you spent together will stay with you throughout your entire life."

"Oh," my son replied, still looking a bit unsure. "No problem."

Aren't I the luckiest dad in the world?

Every year, I planned to keep the reason for the season first and foremost ... and think less about my insecurities. Of course, I'm talking about carving jack-o'-lanterns.

You know how rambunctious teenagers sometimes wander the streets on Halloween night, grabbing people's jack-o'-lanterns off

their front stoops and smashing them in the streets so all that's left
are shards of pumpkin?

That's how mine look *before* they do this.

In fact, last Halloween, I overheard a couple of kids standing
outside my front door saying, "Dang, someone's already been here!"

I can take a perfectly good pumpkin and, in a matter of hours,
make it look like the victim in a slasher movie. And while that may
sound perfect for Halloween, it's no consolation for a child who
originally asked his daddy to carve a clown face.

I'm all thumbs.

Over the years, I tried bowing out of the pumpkin-carving
experience altogether. But unfortunately, my wife put a lot of stock
in us spreading out the newspaper on the kitchen floor and enjoying
an afternoon of old-fashioned jack-o'-lantern making.

Therefore, one year, I stepped up my efforts. Over breakfast, I
announced to the family, "Gang, I hate to be the bearer of bad news,
but all the pumpkins in the country have been recalled. We can't do
any pumpkin carving. I'm heartbroken."

The family looked at me in disbelief.

"It's true," I lied. "Faulty stems. Last Friday, an Akron man
picked up a pumpkin at the grocery store, the stem broke off, and he
lost a toe. Tragic."

My wife called the Agricultural Department … pumpkin carving was back on.

So, I tried plan B.

"Gang, let's do something different and buy professionally
carved pumpkins this year. We'll have the best jack-o'-lanterns on
the street. What do you say?"

The children cried.

"Great, Ken!" my wife exclaimed. "Maybe you'd also like the kids to stay home on Halloween. Maybe FedEx can deliver their treats."

Plan B bit the dust.

So finally, I had to take my wife aside and admit that I was scared and embarrassed to spend one more Halloween season carving pumpkins.

Her reply gave me a lot to think about.

"Ken," she began, "who cares if your pumpkins aren't traditional, or even recognizable? There's something more important to consider here. When you carve a pumpkin, it brings you and your children closer together. That's what the holidays are supposed to be—a time for family and fun. I like your pumpkins. Do you know why?"

I shook my head.

"Because they are a symbol of family togetherness. I'm proud to have your pumpkin on our porch."

"Wow," I said, feeling inspired. "Let's go get some pumpkins."

A few days later, I was raking leaves on the side of the house when I overheard my wife talking to the neighbor about our pumpkins.

"Oh, that one?" my wife said, pointing to *my* jack-o'-lantern on the front stoop. It looked exactly as I'd carved it. "It's Ken's. We think the dog chewed on it."

REFLECTION

Regarding Christmas, how did we get so far from a simple birthday celebration for Jesus? I'm not casting lumps of coal here ... since I am one of the worst offenders (obviously). I struggle to keep Christ in Christmas. I fail 90 percent of the time. There is so much to do, and the expectations surrounding Christmas, Easter, and other holidays are immense. In the end, I often just want to get through it … which is difficult to admit, but there it is.

I loved the holidays as a kid. What was there not to like? Kids just show up and eat feasts or open presents. For adults, the pressures, costs, and labor stack up and often take away whatever joy there is left in the event. And for some people, painful memories of Christmas past equally get in the way.

I am pretty certain God doesn't want that for us.

With that said, however, the holidays do still contain rays of hope. What is true for many is that the holidays bring family together. There is prayer at the table. We attend church services at Christmas and Easter. We give to charities. We sing songs of holy praise. We put nativity scenes on our tables. Sometimes, we forgive. It is on these things that I hope to focus more.

Verse: "Praise be to the God and Father of our Lord Jesus Christ! In his great mercy he has given us new birth into a living hope through the resurrection of Jesus Christ from the dead, and into an inheritance that can never perish, spoil or fade" (1 Pet. 1:3–4).

Further Reading:

Luke 2:1–20

1 Peter 1

Prayer: Lord, there are so many blessings ensconced in the holy traditions of our Christian holidays. Please help me see those and take time with feeling them as well. Often, my perceptions and distractions get in the way of the inherent joy of the birth and resurrection of our Savior Jesus Christ. Open my eyes and heart to these seasonal celebrations. Help me connect with them, share them, and witness Your glory with all who are around me. Please help me remember that the things that unite us far outnumber those few things that divide us. Amen.

CHAPTER SIXTEEN

Trust Is a Five-Letter Word

When you get right down to it, my daughter didn't trust that her mother and I knew what we were doing. As a child, she constantly second-guessed us.

- Are you sure this is the right way to Grandma's house?
- Dad, did you stop the mail before we left for vacation?
- Mom, did you cook this meat long enough?

We got this all the time ... even when she was ten! I think she thought my wife and I were complete morons incapable of safely raising children. Sometimes she would stare at the two of us and gasp, as if amazed we hadn't accidentally killed her (yet).

Of course, I was surprised too ... surprised that after she was born and I held her for the first time, she didn't pop the pacifier out of her mouth and ask if I'd washed my hands first.

I could handle the questions most of the time, but when there was a true emergency or stressful situation, it was a whole different story. Like when I blew a tire on the freeway. My daughter popped her head out of the window as I jacked up the car.

"Dad, have you ever had a flat tire before? Is it safe to raise the car up like that? Isn't that spare tire a little small? It looks like a toy tire. Is that a toy tire? Will that grease come off of your hands? Do you have the wrong tire?"

Meanwhile, cars are whizzing by, and I am trying to concentrate on the task.

"Dad, do you know what you're doing?"

Finally, I just lost it. "No, I don't know what I'm doing," I sarcastically said as I tightened the lug nuts on the spare. "In fact, I'm really only ten years old. I'm not fit to be anyone's parent—you've seen right through me. I've been masquerading as an educated adult male with a mortgage and six mouths to feed because that sounded like more fun than watching cartoons and riding my bike. When I get home, I'm going to clean out the gutters. I'm positively shivering with excitement!"

This did not deter her in the least. "Maybe that's my old Big Wheel tire, and you put it in the trunk by mistake? It looks a lot like my old Big Wheel tire."

It really came down to a lack of trust.

"Daddy, when the Big Wheel tire comes off while we're moving, will the car stop, or will we flip over a few times first?"

If not tires, then …

"Are you sure the doors are locked?" she'd ask. Or "Is the cough syrup you gave me safe?"

I was constantly lecturing her. "Honey, I'm the parent. It is my job to worry about these things—not yours. Relax. Be the kid."

She would nod. "Okay, but I need you to pick me up at the library tonight. Now, I'll be standing to the left of the doorway. To the left ... okay?"

"Okay," I would answer, rubbing my face. "I'll try not to take someone else home by accident. Be sure to keep shooing people away from the left side until I get there."

You'd think that I had accidentally forgotten her at the airport or something to deserve such treatment. I hadn't (I don't think ...).

Of course, unlike with God, not everything can be plain and simple for us mere mortals ... like when a large snowfall closes the schools for several days in our area. At one point, the snow had melted enough that I assumed school would reopen the next day. To double-check, I clicked on the state's school closure website at 8:00 p.m.—there were no new closure announcements. The previous day's closure notice had been posted at 7:00 p.m., so I assumed, since there wasn't a new message, school was back open.

My daughter wasn't as convinced. I had to show her the website.

"Are you sure that's the right site?" she asked.

I ignored her.

At 9:00 p.m., as my daughter kissed me good night, she gave me that distrusting look, again. "Dad, are you sure there's school tomorrow?"

Frustrated, I grabbed a sheet of paper and drew a picture of myself, then ran an arrow from the words "This is your dad." Next, I explained that when I had applied for the job of dad, I assumed all responsibility of being the dad, including overseeing the twenty-four-hour weather reports and school-closure news for the household. Finally, I called Grandma and asked her to tell my daughter who I was.

I presumed that had resolved the issue.

The next morning at six, however, my daughter was at it again. "Dad, do you swear on the Holy Bible that we have school today? I mean, don't you think you should check the website one more time?"

As she said this, her brother walked by. I grabbed his arm and asked, "Son, do you know who I am?"

He nodded. "You're Dad … duh."

I smiled at my daughter: "See? Have a good day at school, sweetie—hurry before the bus leaves."

Thirty minutes later, she and her brother walked into the house with rosy cheeks and snow stuck to their boots.

"School is delayed two hours," my daughter announced. "An old lady who doesn't even have kids told us."

Oh my land!

REFLECTION

And then it dawns on me—every time I worry and fret, fearing the future and losing sleep over the issues in my life, that I'm doing the same to my Father … God. When I freak out, I'm not trusting Him, especially considering He's done nothing but taken good care of me. D'oh!

I hate it when I realize I am a hypocrite!

Verse: "Trust in the LORD with all your heart and lean not on your own understanding" (Prov. 3:5).

Further Reading:

> Psalm 56
> Proverbs 3
> Isaiah 12

Prayer: Lord, I put my trust in You, for You are my Creator, my Father, the One who made me in perfection. Help me to stop trying to control that which is not mine to worry about. I will work today to live in the present, basking in the glory of Your divine grace, letting go of my fear, and just *being* Your child, who is infinitely loved and protected by You. In return, I will help my children, as their mentor and guide in this Christian faith, to do the same. Amen.

CHAPTER SEVENTEEN

Until Death Do Us Part

I was greatly shaken by 9/11. Shortly after it happened, I discussed contingency plans with my wife.

While we stood in our bathroom brushing our teeth for bed, I told her that we needed to:

1. Map out a strategy
2. Decide who would pick the kids up at school in an emergency
3. Buy some plastic sheeting and duct tape
4. Choose a place to huddle in the house
5. Purchase more first-aid supplies for our emergency kit

I didn't want her to think we were in immediate danger, so I also explained exactly where I thought we sat in the pecking order. "If Washington, DC, is a ten, meaning most likely to be attacked by terrorists, our area is probably only a seven."

Then I went to bed.

The next morning, my wife's eyes were bloodshot, and she looked exhausted. I asked her what was wrong.

"What in the world made you think I wanted to have a 'terrorist' conversation just before bed?" she complained.

"It was on my mind. I didn't want to forget."

She yawned. "I lied awake half the night worrying how long it will take the terrorists to get to the sevens." She rubbed her face. "The only way I eventually got to sleep was by singing Mary Poppins songs under my breath."

I walked over and gave her a hug. "I'm sorry, sweetie."

She rolled her eyes. "So, what's your lecture going to be tonight? Terminal-care insurance and funeral plots?"

I felt like such a heel for scaring my wife like that. I'd allowed myself to get caught up in the hysteria of terror warnings and news reports, and I'd forgotten my fundamental job of reassuring my family that everything would be okay. There's nothing wrong with being prepared for the worst, but I didn't need to scare those I loved in the process.

As my wife walked groggily toward her closet, I realized that most guys probably bought the plastic sheeting and duct tape but, when asked about it, told their families it was for home-improvement projects. And they certainly didn't walk around assigning numbers to vulnerable cities and towns—especially their own.

A few days later, a friend of ours stopped by to visit. My wife told her what I'd said.

"I'm in my jammies. It's dark outside. And Ken tells me that we rank in the top third of attackable cities."

Our friend shook her head in disgust. "My husband said we didn't need to worry about things like buying plastic sheeting."

(See what I mean?)

"Well, that's certainly refreshing to hear!" my wife exclaimed, shooting me a dirty look. "So, your husband thinks we're safe?"

"No," she answered. "My husband said that *nothing* we do will do any good, because in a catastrophic emergency, the roving bands of lawless thugs will sack our house and steal our food anyway. And then he went to sleep."

Every so often, I wonder whether, if my wife had to do it all over again, she would rather have married a handyman.

It can't be easy for her being married to me. Our front door hasn't closed correctly in years. In the summer, the slightest breeze pushes it open. This gives our indoor cat the chance to make her getaway, which always concludes with my wife chasing the cat down the street in her bare feet, yelling, "Lucy, come back—you're making Mommy very upset!"

In the winter, the door swells or something (if I were handy, I'd know), which means the dead bolt won't turn without me first muscling the doorknob up and white-knuckling the lock into place. I'm the only one in the house who can do this intricate dance.

A handy guy would know how to correct this problem. A *rich* guy would pay someone to fix it. But my poor wife is left with me … the guy who is always yelling in the summer, "Grab the cat!" and in the winter, "Someone bring Daddy the Bengay!"

It has been difficult for my wife to come to terms with exactly how unhandy I am. When we were first married, I think she thought

I was faking my home-repair ignorance. She didn't believe I couldn't install a ceiling fan or stop the toilet from humming "do-re-mi" whenever it flushed.

I admit this *might* be somewhat because I misrepresented myself on a few occasions while we were first dating. She may have been under the illusion I was handy because I *may have* bragged a little about my background … and because I owned a really nice tool belt. But let's be honest here, societal expectations dictate that men are supposed to be handy. Therefore, it was only because of gender pressure that I told her (lied) that I remodeled homes during summer breaks.

Once we tied the knot, I did my best to keep up the ruse. And to, er, tie a good knot. But soon, my little white lie was out on the sawhorse. I admitted to her that I'd stretched the truth *a little* about my carpentry skills. She said she started to figure that out on her own when I told the clerk at the hardware store that there was a big mistake in lumber—that "all of the two-by-fours in the bin were actually eight feet long, not four."

But that's not the end of our sad little home-repair story. While, after years of marriage, my wife has come to accept (the best she can) my lack of handiness, *I* have not … and not because of societal pressures. Instead, I blame genetic predisposition (in other words, pride—or in *other*, other words, stupidity). Resulting in me trying to fix things, even though I don't have a clue what I am doing.

I'll spare you the gory details, but I truly believe that one of these days I am going to get one of my repair jobs right … and hopefully get the hot water working in the house too.

Please pray for my wife.

However, my wife does get me back ... when I am sick.

Have you heard that old saying "I don't have time to get sick"? My wife subscribes to that motto. But what she really means is that she doesn't have time for *me* to get sick.

It's not that she's cruel. Certainly, when I am feeling ill, she wants me to get better. It's just that she wants me to get better on my own time ... at work, not underfoot. She says she already has enough children to take care of.

I can appreciate that. I'd rather not be babied anyway. So, when I am feeling ill, I suck it up and march on.

Except for the time I had vertigo. I contracted a virus that affected my inner ear. My equilibrium was completely shot. I couldn't see straight, let alone work. Any time I moved, I felt queasy and in danger of emptying my stomach. All I could do was lie down and stare at the wall.

A major symptom like vertigo requires a little caretaking. I'd like to think my wife would have been there for me ... that is, if I hadn't happened to get vertigo the day before our daughter's first birthday party.

Needless to say, my wife wasn't amused.

After all, she had a cake to bake, favors to buy, gifts to wrap, a house to decorate, a dress to sew. At least, that's what I remember her telling me she had to do, as I threw up in the bathroom.

Even with birthday parties to plan, I suppose the Florence Nightingales of the marriage world would have still brought their husbands hot chicken soup for lunch.

My wife brought me the can.

"Chicken noodle?" I asked.

"Beef barley."

I took one look at the can and reassured her that I would be okay. "It's *probably* not my last meal on earth."

That didn't go over well. Her lips started to quiver, and then she cried. She told me how far behind she was in making the party perfect for our daughter. She talked about the pressure to have the house clean for her mother. She listed all the toys that needed assembly. And she wondered how these things would get done without me able to help.

So, I did what any husband with even half a heart would do in this situation. Out of guilt, I stood up and told her I would help.

Then I fell on my face.

She sobbed. "And I can't get the Jell-O to set!"

I rolled onto my back and stared blankly at the ceiling. "Just a minor setback, sweetheart. If I can just get to my knees ..."

She stopped crying and knelt down to me. Her voice was soft and sweet. "Get back into bed, Ken. You're really sick. Truly. I'll manage somehow."

Our eyes met. She braved a grin. I knew she meant what she said.

I propped myself onto my elbow. "Honey, I want to help. Go put the leash on the dog—he can drag me into the living room to assemble the toys."

She dabbed her eyes. "Really? Oh, Ken. Thank you!" She paused at the door. "Could you also dust the baseboards on your way down the hall?"

I closed my eyes and nodded.

How did she do that?

My wife and I have had several conversations that somehow all ended with me proclaiming, "I'm *not* a girl!"

Let me explain with an anecdote.

One year, my family and I went on vacation. Prior to our departure, a friend of ours, who was in a period of transition, asked if he could stay at our house while we were gone. While I had no worries telling my friend that that was okay, my wife transformed into Mrs. Clean at the news and scrubbed our house from one end to the other. Four days later, the children and I loaded into the car for our vacation with luggage and smiles. My wife climbed in with dishpan hands.

Needless to say, as my wife obsessed over the house and what my friend might think if he saw the vacuum patterns in the living room running the wrong way, I did what I always do—I laughed at her. Especially when, as we pulled away from the house, she told me that she got everything done that she wanted, including ironing the pillowcases on our bed.

"Ironing the pillowcases?" I chuckled. "Why does my friend get ironed pillowcases and I don't?"

To which my wife replied tersely, "I always iron our pillowcases. You didn't notice?"

Do women even notice that? Don't answer that!

And this is why a *guy* wrote the book *Men Are from Mars, Women Are from Venus*. He was just trying to let his wife know why he didn't notice the pillowcases were ironed.

No matter how many times I say it, however, my wife still doesn't understand that I'm not a girl. Especially in terms of how we communicate. Here are some classic examples.

> 1. When my wife returned from her Weight Watchers meeting and told me that she'd lost a pound, I'd usually say, "Nice job." But what she expected to hear (thinking that I was a girl) was "You worked really hard to lose that pound, didn't you? I would have guessed you'd lost five pounds. How do you *feel* about the week ahead? Are you nervous you'll gain weight, considering all the commitments and expectations people have on you? I bet all men, and your mom, just don't understand how hard this is for you, do they? Tissue?"
>
> 2. When I came home from work and my wife said the kids were driving her crazy, and I said, "Let's sell them," what she was expecting me to say was "Honey, even with the grape jelly stuck to your face and that paper airplane in your hair, you look ravishing. Here, let me make dinner."

Contrary to popular opinion, however, men do not think that women are men or should sound like men. We don't expect women to understand how we feel about *Die Hard*, dark beer, or fantasy football.

But then again, I am pretty sure women aren't too worried that they don't sound like men anyway.

Of course, when I was a young man, contemplating my life as a future husband and father, never once did I imagine pulling wax off the mustache area of my wife.

Pulling weeds? I could see doing that. Changing a tire? Cooking? Those, I figured, would fall on my list of duties.

But salon services? I think if I had insight into that as a twenty-year-old, I might have considered a prenuptial agreement that restricted the removal of anything follicular.

I remember my first waxing as if it were yesterday. I was minding my own business when my wife appeared before me with a sheen of yellow goop across the top of her lip.

"Did you just kiss toxic waste?" I asked, inching away from her.

She threw me a smile. "I need you to count to three and rip this wax off," she explained. Then, giving a shudder, she added, "But do it quick—like you're ripping off a Band-Aid."

"That's okay," I replied. "I'm not good with Band-Aids. And besides, I feel kind of funky now."

Even as I said those words, I knew I had no choice.

My wife said it was a simple procedure. "Ken, you just grab the edge of the wax and pull quickly forward. It's not rocket science."

That was true, I told her. "But at least when you're working with rockets, you get to wear protective clothing."

We must have gone around and around in that conversation for thirty minutes. All the while, my wife stood there looking like Groucho Marx with a skin affliction. Finally, she lowered the boom.

"Ken, it costs $45 for the salon to do my waxing. If you do it, it's like 50 cents in wax—period."

It's just like my wife to know my pressure points.

"Fine," I said. "But I want a tip. And I don't do Brazilian waxes."

Nervously, I approached the wax. It curled slightly at the end so I could grip and tear. Squeezing the wax between by thumb and finger, I started the countdown.

"Three … two …"

"*Wait!*" my wife screamed.

I froze. "What?"

"One easy and quick motion, okay?"

I rolled my eyes. "Sweetie, trust me: you'll get what you paid for."

Riiiiiiip!

After the screams died down (mostly mine), we examined the reddened area above her mouth.

"Not bad," she said. "See, that wasn't hard."

I have to admit: I did a good job. I glanced at my wife. "Now, what are we going to do about those bangs?"

Since that first time, I have probably deforested my wife's lip twenty times. I guess word of my services got around too, because my daughter began appearing at my side from time to time with goop on her lip. Only, she tended to spread the wax like she was appearing next in the center ring in a tiny Ringling Brothers car.

I suppose it was the least I could do for the two girls in my life. When I was twenty, such things may not have been what I imagined I would be doing as a father and husband. But in an odd way, I wouldn't trade these small, intimate moments for anything.

In fact, maybe I should open my own studio. I could call it Chez Ken.

I can't believe I just wrote that.

If my wife is from Venus, then I can assure you, Mars is a much colder planet.

She and I can't ever agree on the heat setting in our car. I'm situated behind the steering wheel turning down the temperature, while she's sitting in the passenger seat turning it back up a hundred degrees. I'm always hot, and she's always cold.

To say we've had our share of arguments while rambling down the highway would be an understatement ... as I am sure my children will share with their therapists one of these days.

> Me: Honey, tell me when to turn because I can't see.
> The skin appears to have melted off my forehead.
> My wife: L-l-lucky. I c-c-can't f-f-feel my feet.

How do two people with completely different bodily systems resolve this issue? What do you do when one person feels baked and the other one feels frozen? Is there a solution, aside from taking two cars?

I don't know the answers to those questions, so I rely on stealth.

Simply put, when my wife looks out the car window, closes her eyes to rest, or whips her head around to inform the children that they aren't too old to be put up for adoption, I reach over to the heater control and turn it off.

By the time my wife is facing forward again, I am happily driving without any further concerns of heat stroke.

This clandestine temperature control works 99 percent of the time ... until my wife realizes she can see her breath (or so she claims).

> My wife: I'm freezing! Hey! Who turned off the
> heat?
> Me: Kids? Your mother just asked you a question!
> Who did it?

Unfortunately, what's good for the roasted gander is also good for the cold duck. Only, instead of stealth maneuvers, my wife employs a more sophisticated technique: guilt.

She likes to remind me that she has thin blood and a slow metabolism and that our AAA membership doesn't include emergency airlifts in the case of front-seat hypothermia. I usually stop fiddling with the heat setting after she lays it on thick like that. That is, until I develop heat blisters. (Or she looks away.)

I'm not sure we'll ever resolve this problem, unless I am willing to sell our cars and buy a more expensive model that includes heated seats and individual climate settings for both front-seat riders.

And so, our lives continue ...

My wife: I'm cold.

Me: You said that twenty minutes ago.

My wife: No, I said, "I am ...," and then my jaw froze shut.

Me: You don't appear to be having difficulty speaking now.

My wife: That's because I splashed your latte on my face.

Me: Yeah, well, don't touch the temperature gauge—I'm hot as hades.

My wife: Ha! You aren't even sweating.

Me: That's because I'm driving in only my underwear.

My wife: And?

Me: And I think that bus driver next to us is writing down my license plate.

If the government really wanted to strengthen marriages, it would put marriage counselors at highway rest stops.

REFLECTION

I love being married. My wife and I started dating in our junior year of high school. Four children, a mortgage, jobs, extended families, pets, hundreds of challenges, and thirty-seven years (as of this writing) later, we are still together.

Our secret?

1. The understanding that the irritations I have with her are equal to the number of ways I irritate

her. Seriously. Love, companionship, children, camaraderie, and history aside, marriage works when both partners stop trying to change each other; when they accept their differences and understand the fact that neither of them is holier than the other. In other words, I want to be loved despite my limitations as a husband, and my wife wants to be loved in the same way.

2. We are always on the same side. In other words, it is the two of us against the children.

3. Marriage isn't always easy, but it helps to remember that giving up would just mean repeating the same problems with someone else.

4. Complimenting each other. Listening and repeating back. Talking problems out, not ignoring them.

5. Working to improve ourselves inside and out, as a mark of respect to the relationship.

6. Knowing that God brought us together for a reason, and we hopefully have fifty-plus more years together to discover more of why. Have faith in Him by showing faith in each other. Remember, it's about the journey—detours and potholes included.

Verse: "'Haven't you read,' he replied, 'that at the beginning the Creator "made them male and female," and said, "For this reason a man will leave his father and mother and be united to his wife, and the two will become one flesh"? So they are no longer two, but one

flesh. Therefore what God has joined together, let no one separate'"
(Matt. 19:4–6).

Further Reading:

Mark 10
Ephesians 4

Prayer: I am blessed in so many ways, Lord. Help me appreciate that
every moment, especially for the love You have bestowed upon me
when You brought my spouse and me together. I do not want to ever
take that for granted. Thank You for Your blessings. Amen.

CHAPTER EIGHTEEN

Smells Like Teen Spirit

Nearly twenty years ago, I saw a story out of Florida about the couple who went on strike … against their kids.

Cat and Harlan Barnard moved out of their Deltona, Florida, home and into a tent on their front lawn to protest the lack of respect and help they received around the house from their seventeen-year-old son and twelve-year-old daughter.[3]

I am sure most parents of teenagers had one of two reactions when they heard this story. One group of moms and dads were startled by the Barnards' behavior. They didn't understand how the Barnards could abandon their own children, especially a teenager and a near-teenager who were at that age when they needed a parent's support more than ever.

The second group of parents with teenagers reacted entirely different. These moms and dads sent the Barnards greeting cards that read "Congratulations" and "Way to go" and "Is there room in your tent for me?"

Why the two groups? It has, scientists tell us, something to do with genetics. The first group of parents gave birth to children with low levels of the "teen gene." These parents criticized the Barnards because they had delightful teenagers living in their homes. Teens who wanted nothing else than to impress their parents with "inside voices," a gallant spirit, and the English language. These parents couldn't begin to see why anyone would want to move out on a teenager.

The second group of parents didn't feel this way because they were raising teenagers with adequate amounts of the teen gene. These parents felt a solidarity with the Barnards because they, too, had teens who left their things strung around the house and who needed frequent introductions to the dishwasher, the laundry room, and how to flush a toilet. These folks hoped the Barnards would be named *Time* magazine's "Person(s) of the Year."

After this story broke, my wife and I discussed going on strike too. Only, in our plan, it was the children who would move into the tent. Sure, you could argue that my kids could've learned a bigger lesson if they'd been confronted with the responsibility of keeping an entire household running. But let's be honest, my kids wouldn't even be able to keep the tent clean.

I wonder if other parents in the second group fantasized about walking the picket line after reading the Barnards' story. I wonder if they printed out the article and pasted it to their teenagers' bathroom mirrors. I wonder if my son ever got tired of me calling the Barnards his new godparents.

But I also wonder what the first group of parents took from this story. Did they realize how good they had it to be raising well-behaved teenagers? Would they have agreed to trade kids with me for a while?

After all, here is how many of the conversations with my teen-agers went:

>Me: How was your day?
>
>Teenager: Fine.
>
>Me: Oh. What did you do today?
>
>Teenager: Nothing.
>
>Me: Oh. Nothing as in something, or nothing as in you just got out of a coma?
>
>Teenager: Nothing as in nothing.
>
>Me: So what's new at school? And please don't say "nothing."
>
>Teenager: Not much.
>
>Me: You know, you can discuss anything with me.
>
>Teenager: Sure.
>
>Me: Sure, as in you'd like to do that?
>
>Teenager:
>
>Me: Are you hungry?
>
>Teenager: No.
>
>Me: Because I am going to the kitchen, and I could bring you something. I don't mind. Can I get you something?
>
>Teenager: Chips.
>
>Me: Chips. Excellent. All the way to the kitchen and back, I'm going to savor your use of a new word. Chips … chips … chips.
>
>(Running into my second teenager by the refrigerator)
>
>Me: Hi. What are you looking for in the fridge?

Teenager: Stuff.

Me: Are you hungry?

Teenager: Duh.

Me: How was your day today? And please don't say "fine."

Teenager:

Me: You know, you can discuss anything with me.

Teenager: Whatever.

Me: Sure, whatever you want.

Teenager: I meant, whatever, as in whatever.

Me: Wow. That was six words you just used. Your brother just said the word *chips*. Is it Father's Day? (pause) I'm headed back to the family room. Is there a message I can give your brother?

Teenager:

(Back at the couch)

Me: Hey, I was just chatting with your sister by the refrigerator. We had a good talk. Here are your chips. I wasn't sure if you wanted corn chips, potato chips, or the soy chips, so I brought all three.

Teenager: Thanks.

Me: So which one would you have chosen?

Teenager: Of what?

Me: The chips.

Teenager: Corn.

Me: Great. I can now add that to the things I know about you. That was an easy question, wasn't it? What's your second favorite type of chip?

Teenager: Potato.

Me: Potato—neat. So, which one of your friends is taking drugs?

Teenager:

Me: So soy is your least favorite, huh?

Teenager: Whatever.

I stopped by my son's school one year. Not to have a conference with his teachers or to volunteer for a booster club project. I was there to confiscate his gym clothes.

They hadn't been home since the first day of school. My wife and I had asked our son many times about these clothes, but each time, he claimed they were doing just fine.

"Fine as in 'smelling fresh'?" I asked him. "Or, fine as in 'a nice maggot family is living in the armpit'?"

Our son assured us that he didn't sweat, and therefore, the clothes didn't need a wash.

I, on the other hand, had visions of green noxious gas seeping from his gym locker and a big fat fine from the EPA. So I finally decided to take matters into my own hands. I grabbed a long pole and headed for the school.

I checked in at the main office, and the secretary told me that other moms and dads had been in recently on similar missions.

I was relieved to hear I wasn't the only one.

She smiled. "It's just about this time every year that parents stop believing their sons will ever bring home their gym clothes."

I admitted I was one of them. "You know," I said, "when I was a kid, we used to get paddled by the coaches if we didn't take our gym clothes home."

"Yes, well, we tend to frown on that these days," the secretary said. "After all, it's our position at this school that boys and girls should learn personal responsibility and pride."

"I suppose," I replied. "So, what's your position on pestilence?"

Next, I asked the secretary to point me in the direction of the boys' locker room.

She cringed. "Are you prepared to do this?"

I nodded bravely. "I brought a bag with me. It hermetically seals."

When I reached the gym, my son was walking out of the locker room in his school clothes. I told him to march right back inside and bring out his shorts, T-shirt, and socks. As I stood outside the locker room, a small towheaded kid asked me what I was doing.

"I'm taking my son's gym clothes home to have them burned."

The boy nodded as if he had heard the same threats from his parents. "Every time I wear my gym clothes, they make my nose burn."

When my son walked out with his clothes, he held them at arm's length, delicately pinched between two fingers. I made him admit to me that the clothes could use a washing.

"Okay. They're bad."

I creased my forehead. "So why haven't you taken them home?"

"I keep forgetting," he explained.

"But doesn't the smell, the rancor, the grossness remind you?"

"Yes—while I'm wearing them. But I have gym in the morning."

"So?"

"So, the lingering odor on my skin leaves my body by lunch."

After he placed his gym clothes in my bag, I stopped by the principal's office and put in a request that next quarter my son have gym in the last period of the day.

Mall shopping is not what it used to be. Namely because I didn't used to do it. I've shunned malls most of my life. That all changed the day my sweet little daughter became a teenager … and needed a ride.

I learned to follow her around the stores, trying not to do anything that might embarrass her (per her orders).

A teenage girl's shopping habits are baffling to me. They have a system I simply don't understand. There's no efficiency to it. It's perfectly okay in their world to spend four hours walking from store to store (backtracking often), trying on a hundred different outfits, and then leaving with just a new pair of socks.

In other words, they beg and beg to be taken to the mall because they have nothing to wear to school, and then they return home with one, maybe two items (three if you include barrettes). Does that make sense to anyone?

Not many dads understand this process. I know—I've met many of my fellow befuddled fathers at the mall. There's an entire subculture of fathers there in the evenings, all leaning exhaustedly on clothing racks, listening to hip-hop, and praying a plus-size mannequin will fall on their heads and put them out of their misery.

We shuffle alone from one teenybopper store to the next ... acknowledging the other dads with weary eyes, except for the rare occasions when a store not only has chairs but has two of them side by side. In those cases, our conversations go something like this:

> Dad 1: I miss the days when just moms took their kids to the mall.
> Dad 2: I miss the Home Depot.

Of course, I was surprised to see other dads there. I say *surprised* only because I thought I was the world's biggest pushover, giving in to my daughter. Apparently, I'm not the only one. I saw one dad with not only his daughter but also her friends. I'd need sedatives to do that.

All in all, this is just one more place that the gender boundaries have blurred for men and women in the twenty-first century. Like many other traditional "mom-only" activities (such as cooking, cleaning, and midnight feedings for the baby), we can now add shopping at the mall as both a dad and a mom responsibility.

I guess I just have one thing to say about that: guys, we really need better places to hide.

I do not, however, drive my son to the mall—or anywhere else, for that matter. He got his driver's license years ago. And I have the anxious memories to prove it.

Teaching a child to drive is one of the many wonderful rites of passage in parenting … as is screaming in the front passenger seat and praying that the airbags work.

Until I handed my son the keys to my truck, I had forgotten just how many things drivers are expected to do all at once, such as staying on the road, signaling before turns, and applying the brakes instead of hitting a curb.

It's all a daze now, but I think our first lesson (in a fairly deserted and new construction area) went something like this:

> Me: Okay, son, put your foot on the brake and start the engine. Good, but next time, let's not enter the street until you have looked for oncoming traffic. Okay, fine, fine, we *do* want to stop at stop signs, though. Turn here. Yes, braking would probably be a good thing right about now. *Umph!* Okay, go ahead and back off the sidewalk.
>
> (I turned to my son and told him that learning to drive isn't the easiest thing in the world. He climbed back behind the wheel, and we continued.)
>
> Me: Let's try it again. Actually, once the engine is on, we don't need to turn the key anymore. Now, check both ways. Watch your speed. Fine. Okay, there's a roundabout up ahead. Good, but when you hear your passenger's head bang into the door window like that, it's a fair indication that it's time to slow down. Okay, go ahead and back off the roundabout.

(Notice how calm I was? I think I did a decent job of encouraging my son on his first day ... until, that is, we entered real traffic on the drive home, and I started coaching.)

Me: *Too close ... Stay in your lane ... Slow down ... Mommy!*

(I understand that millions of parents before me have taught their children to drive. I get that.)

Me: Try to keep an equal distance between the center line and the curb. Good, turn here. Now, the light up ahead is red, so we should start applying some brake about now. About now. Now, please. *Stop!* Go ahead and back off the curb.

We eventually made it home in one piece. And I was proud of both my son and myself.

Then, on our second day of driving lessons, my son was pulled over by a police officer for suspicion of drunk driving. True story.

Still, when he turned sixteen, he passed his driver's test. Since then, he has been on the road solo ... God bless us all. I can report that in the first ninety-six hours he had his driver's license, he managed to go through three tanks of gas, run his battery down after leaving his headlights on, and even pop his front right tire hitting a curb.

I should've opened a tow truck business.

I had mixed emotions about my son driving ... and not just because of the car mishaps. It was great that I didn't have to drive him to the three soccer practices and game each week for the forty-eight weeks out of the year he played. It was cool that I didn't have to get him to his school events, which he invariably announced at the last minute. I was thrilled that he could drive himself to his own doctor appointments, sports events, and the bazillion times he just hung out with friends. I was a free man! Or was I?

All the free time I gained, I filled up with worrying. I knew the day would come when he'd leave the nest. I just hoped it wouldn't be at forty-five miles an hour inside a vehicle licensed to kill. I didn't like the loss of control I felt. I didn't like that my son could have a serious accident. I didn't like the DMV dude who gave my son a passing grade.

Perhaps you're thinking, *He went through exactly what I am experiencing.* Perhaps you're chuckling that I acted as if I were the first dad to experience the "new-driver jitters." I wonder: Does the feeling ever go away? Even when your child is twenty-nine and fully independent, are you ever comfortable that he or she is out in the big world driving on his or her own?

I suspect not.

To combat my fears in those first ninety-six hours when my son was a licensed driver, I found myself telling him as many dangers about the road as I could. While making my son a peanut butter and jelly sandwich, I told him that forty-three thousand people die each year on the highways. As I congratulated him on his successful math test, I said, "Always remember—safety is a cheap and effective insurance policy." And while we enjoyed a belly laugh over an episode of *The Office*, I explained that there's nothing worse than flying through your windshield at eighty miles an hour because you forgot to buckle up.

Yep, I had a lot more where those came from, let me tell you. I just hope when he's thirty he's still listening.

Parenting is full of these exciting moments. One of my favorites is trying to turn out the lights and lock the doors downstairs before going to bed, and then praying they stay that way. I really like that game … next to reasoning with a teenager.

Closing down for the evening is not a simple task. The challenge at my home was always locking the doors and shutting off the lights before there was no longer a reason to go to sleep … say, for example, because it was morning and I was late for work.

There were many reasons why closing up shop was difficult. For example, when my kids heard me yell, "It's bedtime—everyone in their rooms," they had the sudden urge to do something else, like flip on all the lights and look for their retainers, or make their lunches for the next day, or call me from their cell phones.

> Me: Hello?
> Child: Dad?
> Me: Yes? Where are you?
> Child: Downstairs. I'm going to make waffles. Want any?

Once, as I climbed into bed, a child got stuck on the roof.

I often pondered what the children were thinking when they saw me turn out the lights and close the garage doors.

> Child: Hmmm, Dad has turned everything off and gone to bed. I'd better hurry and rearrange my entire bedroom. I've always wanted to remove my closet door.

I found myself mumbling a lot from under the covers.

> Me: Didn't I just tell everyone to go to bed?
>
> My wife: Do I smell waffles?

It was the last-minute planning, mostly, that delayed the end of the day. Namely, my children waited until a nanosecond before their bedtime to prepare for sleep. It was as if nighttime took them completely by surprise.

Teenagers are the worst. The younger kids go to bed early. Teens think they are the night patrol.

I'm drifting off to sleep when the hall lights flip on full blast.

> Me (throwing a pillow over my face): Whoever turned on the lights better be bleeding or just figured out the answer to world peace and can't wait until morning to share it. If not, I'm removing all the light bulbs in this house, permanently.
>
> Teen: I need you to sign my permission slip.

Me: Why didn't you ask me to do that earlier?

Teen: I forgot.

Me: And yet somehow you always remember to have me sign things when I am lying here on my back with the bedroom lights out. Doesn't your teacher ever wonder why my signature is always crooked?

Maybe I should've turned my house into a 7-Eleven.

Mostly, though, I should've stopped engaging with the teenagers.

Hello, my name is Ken Swarner, and I am an engager.

Not in the marrying sense— I've done that only once. Rather, as a parent, I tended to "engage" with my teenagers. In other words, I spent a lot of time talking to myself.

As an engager, I tried to reason with my teenagers. I also argued with them, articulated my viewpoints, and if need be, made PowerPoint presentations.

If anyone was keeping score, the tally would be dad—0, children—12,354.

My wife told me I needed to stop doing this, or at the very least, to stop keeping score. I wish I could have. I tried twelve-step programs, going cold turkey, and taping my mouth shut, but alas, I couldn't get beyond the hope that I *might* be able to rationalize with them one of these days.

Don't laugh—it could happen.

I always had good intentions when I entered a dialogue with my teenagers. I usually spent fifteen minutes discussing a particular decision in a calm and sane manner. This usually got me nowhere, but like my wife often says, "I'll give you this, Ken, you are persistent."

She also enjoys saying, "Now if only you could pick up your clothes as consistently."

It's true; I am a dogged engager.

One time, my daughter wanted me to drop her off at the mall with her friend ... and then she wanted me to leave them there. I gave my nine-point dissertation on why this was not a good idea.

She didn't like any of my answers. Therefore, the next hour went something like this:

> Me: And that is why I am making this decision.
> Daughter: You are being unreasonable.
> Me: No, I'm not unreasonable. I have a responsibility to parent you so that you are safe.
> Daughter: How is this dangerous?
> Me: It's unsupervised.
> Daughter: (agitated) Don't you trust me by now?
> Me: I do trust you. But in this case—
> Daughter: (crying loudly) You want me to be miserable!

And so forth and so forth and so forth ... on and on and on.

My wife, on the other hand, does not do this. She was a middle school teacher, so she "got" that you can't reason with a teenager any more than you can reason with a hungry lion, a stampede of bulls, or a mother-in-law.

So, she cuts right to the chase in conversations like the one above.

Mom: Yes, that's right, I do want to make your life
miserable. Now go to your room.

Daughter: (shocked) *What?* At least Dad talked
about it!

Mom: That may be true, but your dad is also right
now wrapping his face with duct tape.

My wife is my hero.

And then there are the one-sided memos I used to leave for my
teenager ...

Monday

Son,

*Our house was toilet-papered sometime during the night, probably
by someone you know. I say that because I doubt my coworkers had time
to do it, considering the big project we have going on this week. I'll be
home late, but if you have time in your busy schedule (in between eating,
playing video games, sleeping, eating, and playing video games), could
you remove the TP, trim the front hedge, and rake the leaves that blew
over from Mrs. McCurdy's yard last fall?*

Love, Dad

*P.S. Put the leaves in the compost
pile, not under the house.*

Tuesday

Son,

Did you and your friends have enough to eat yesterday? I noticed half a cookie left in the bare cupboard, and I couldn't sleep all night, worried that one of your buddies might be home, doubled over with hunger pains. What's for brunch today? Any chance you could eat at a friend's house the rest of the week? By the way, I'm happy that you and your buddies found my high school yearbook so amusing. Just out of curiosity, who wrote "dork" next to my picture?

Dad

P.S. I know it's difficult to see the garbage cans and leaves through the toilet paper hanging in front of the windows, but they are all still there (just in case you were wondering)!

Wednesday

Son,

Thanks for trimming the hedge like I asked. I didn't realize, however, what a visual artist you were. How long have you been able to create shapes out of bushes with a hedge trimmer? Was that a middle finger? Maybe we should sign you up for art classes, landscaping, or summer camp! I hacked that finger off late last night. Oh, the bikini babes are gone too … as is most of the hedge now!

Dad

P.S. Little bits of toilet paper are now blowing down the street like confetti.

Thursday

Son,

Thanks for picking up the toilet paper (finally!). Any chance you could remove the huge pile of it off the front lawn? Your little brother tried to roll it into a snowman.

Dad

P.S. I was shocked to hear you and your friends up so early this morning. I was also surprised to find that you took my car. Well, got to go, the taxi is here.

Friday

Son,

Imagine my surprise when I saw that the leaves were finally raked off the lawn yesterday (and I didn't even have to remind you a seventh time—pinch me!). First the hedge, then the toilet paper, and now this. It was one of the proudest moments of my adult life.

That is, until Mrs. McCurdy next door informed me that you put the leaves back in her yard. I am aware that technically the leaves blew over from her yard in the first place, and the note you tacked to her door clearly spelled that out in no uncertain terms (the picture of the police arresting her next time it happens certainly drove the point home).

But I must raise two issues with the letter. Number one, it's "leaves," not "leafs"; and second, why did you sign my name?

Dad

P.S. You start summer school on Monday.

REFLECTION

Ah, teenagers—just one more opportunity for us to read the book of Job to find ways to cope.

Their pushing away at times seems mostly about the biological forces God put in place to make sure our children move out when the time comes. They need to fly from the nest, and in order to do so, they need confidence to enter the adult world. And this self-assurance usually shows up in the form of said teenager thinking he or she knows more than his or her parents.

It is our job, I think, to give them the room they need to fail, regroup, try again, and hopefully succeed. Or at least learn they can handle not succeeding. And repeating this over and over. The name of the game is resiliency. Are teenagers able to handle the ups and downs of life? Do they know where to find the resources they'll need? Do they know they can ask for and receive guidance from the Holy Spirit?

That last part is a rough process for some families. Often, the transition from child to teenager takes some patience as our children sometimes go through periods of rejecting God. Some still have faith, but they would rather sleep in on a Sunday morning than go to church. Others believe they no longer need a faith in God.

Having done it different ways, I have a few recommendations about teenagers:

> 1. Make them go to church with you every week, even though they have a grumpy face … or worse. Don't give up. And remember, dads, from chapter 3: you have to go too!

2. Talk about God and your faith with your teenagers. Speak in their terms—acknowledge their pressures and tell them how God can help. The more you incorporate your beliefs in your everyday conversations with them, the better. They are listening ... even when they say they aren't.

3. Pray for them. Three of my four children are already adults. One is a self-proclaimed atheist, and the other doesn't go to church but hasn't ruled faith out in her life. I'm not giving up. I talk about God and prayer with both of them. They listen. I pray. We'll see.

Finally, remember, church is full of people who were once teenagers too. There is always hope.

Verse: "No temptation has overtaken you except what is common to mankind. And God is faithful; he will not let you be tempted beyond what you can bear. But when you are tempted, he will also provide a way out so that you can endure it" (1 Cor. 10:13).

Further Reading:

Proverbs 22
John 14

Prayer: Lord, I am reminded today that You always welcome me back into Your loving arms regardless of my errors. Therefore, I am to be the same kind of loving father with my children. I ask to be guided in my quest to love my teenagers unconditionally while I also gently remind them about the awesome power of prayer, forgiveness, and hope. Please, heavenly Father, watch over all teenagers. Please help them be safe and sound. Amen.

The Other Family

Everyone knows one … the perfect family. The flawless mom, dad, kids, and pets who seemingly exist solely to remind you and the world that your family isn't nearly as accomplished.

They belong to your church. They attend your school. They stand on the sidelines of the baseball game. They are like hapless stalkers, and no restraining order in the world can protect your ego.

They are also the nicest people in the world (of course), and therefore, who could wish anything bad to happen to them … out loud?

We all know a family like this, and yet we rarely understand how they do it. How come they have the perfect kids? How come they drive the perfect cars and live in the perfect homes? How come it's them and not us?

For my mother-in-law, it is the Thomas family. The Thomases are retired. They have three children. Their oldest son retired a multi-millionaire. Another child made it to the Olympic Trials. Other Thomas children and grandchildren have served as missionaries, taken in foster children, taught in inner-city schools … and always call their mom on Mother's Day.

No one in the Thomas clan has gone to jail, been divorced, or cried in front of the school counselor, professing, "I don't know what to do with this child."

When something bad happens to my wife's family, her mother always laments, "How come this never happens to Beverly Thomas?" It's as if my mother-in-law believes the Thomases do this to her on purpose.

Inevitably, someone in the family will say something like "I bet the Thomases have skeletons in their closet" or "I'm sure something is wrong with them."

But what if they are, in fact, perfect? What if my mother-in-law has a family of flawed individuals, and they don't? What if there really is nothing in the Thomas family to make her feel better about her own?

I have struggled with these issues over the years as well. I look at my own family—my wife and kids, our crazy cat—and it's obvious we have faced many challenges, some of them quite public. Believe me, no one who knows us is sitting at home right now, bent out of shape because the perfect Swarners share the same neighborhood.

But seriously, why worry about the Thomas family? Pride? Have we learned nothing? Are we destined to repeat these lessons over and over? I can assure you, God does not want me or anyone else to make these comparisons. He wants us to focus on Jesus, not the Thomas family!

One thing I've learned is that God has a plan for each of us. He has a reason why the Thomas family is who they are and why I've sat in the principal's office as many times as I have. I may not get to know the reason fully right now, but if I continue to pray and reflect, to talk to God, to read the Gospels, and to discern God's wishes for me, maybe I'll get closer and closer to the truth—the real Truth.

I sincerely thank my children for the ways in which I've found God through the lessons and challenges they've brought me. I am a better person for their faith in me. I pray that they will find their strength in Jesus.

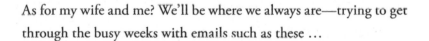

As for my wife and me? We'll be where we always are—trying to get through the busy weeks with emails such as these …

Monday

Sweetheart,

I had an early staff meeting this morning. Your son has soccer today—he's not exactly sure where his shin pads are. We're out of milk. Can you stop at the grocery store on your way home tonight? Have you seen my raincoat? I couldn't find it anywhere, so I had to take yours.

Hugs and kisses,
Allison

Monday

Honey,

Stop at the grocery store? You thought I'd have time to stop at the grocery store? I told the kids to use your soy milk instead. They didn't like it. I'll wash the spit-up out of the sink tonight. I don't have time now because I just spent the morning digging in the camping stuff looking for alternative rain gear. I'll probably be the only one at work today dashing into the office with the words "Give a Hoot—Don't Pollute" stamped on the front of a plastic orange poncho for children. I'm home late tonight. Pray for sun.

Love,
Ken
P.S. No sign of the shin pads—I found something that will work instead.

Tuesday

Ken,

When I picked our son up at soccer practice yesterday, the coach seemed a little confused that our son had pot holders stuffed in his socks. I told him you probably had a negative reaction to your cough syrup that morning. Did you know your daughter needed a poster board and five spools of yarn by noon today? She said you did. I'll sneak out just before lunch and run them over to her.

Love,
Allison
P.S. Still can't find my raincoat. The kids claim they haven't seen it. I suspect they are holding it ransom for the milk.

Tuesday

Allison,

I'll try to get the milk and shin pads, but remember, I have to lead a Boy Scout hike tonight. I can only imagine how my "Don't Give a

Hoot" poncho is going to go over with the teenagers. I'm out of clean underwear ... I'm going commando.

Love,

Ken

P.S. I hope I don't end up unconscious in the hospital today.

Wednesday

Hey,

Before you went hiking commando, you should have checked to see if we had skin ointment. I hope you are walking normally soon. You may want to add ointment to the grocery list, right after milk, shin pads, and laundry detergent.

Allison

Wednesday

Yo,

I penciled in grocery shopping on my to-do list ... right next to breathing. The kids just dropped a tub of yogurt. Gotta go!

Ken

Thursday

I'll be home late tonight—after the PTA meeting. I noticed you finally made it to the grocery store. Yay! Of course, you forgot milk ... and shin pads. The kids used Coca-Cola on their Cheerios this morning. Boy, yogurt can sure travel far. I found the cat licking the dining room chair this morning. Day 4—no raincoat.

Allison

Thursday

When we find your raincoat, I'm thinking about smothering myself to death in it.

Ken

Friday

I found my raincoat. It was hanging where it is supposed to be … go figure—that's a first. The coach asked me last night if we could get our son shin pads by game time on Saturday. I assured him that we would. Sending your son to practice yesterday in Moon Boots didn't go over well. All I want for Christmas this year is milk.

Love,
Allison

Friday

Medic!

Notes

1. Council of Europe, European Population Committee, "The Demographic Characteristics of Linguistic and Religious Groups in Switzerland," 1994–1999, table 9, https://rm.coe.int/16804fb7b1.

2. Sun Tzu, *The Art of War* (Mineola, NY: Ixia, 2019), 31–32.

3. "Kids May Celebrate as Parents Revolt," *Sarasota Herald-Tribune*, December 13, 2004, www.heraldtribune.com/story/news/2004/12/13/kids-may-celebrate-as-parents-revolt/28827318007/; and "Parents Strike against Lazy Kids," SBS News, August 22, 2013, www.sbs.com.au/news/parents-strike-against-lazy-kids.